FAST FORWARD 1

CLASSBOOK

Val Black
Maggy McNorton
Angi Malderez
Sue Parker

OXFORD UNIVERSITY PRESS

Oxford University Press, Walton Street, Oxford OX2 6DP

Oxford
New York   Toronto   Melbourne   Auckland
Petaling Jaya   Singapore   Hong Kong   Tokyo
Delhi   Bombay   Madras   Calcutta   Karachi
Nairobi   Dar es Salaam   Cape Town

and associated companies in
Berlin   Ibadan

Oxford English and the *Oxford English logo* are trade marks of
Oxford University Press

ISBN 0 19 432300 5

© Oxford University Press 1986

First published 1986
Fifth impression 1989

Set in Rockwell Light by VAP Group Ltd., Kidlington
Printed in Hong Kong

*The publishers would like to thank the following for their
permission to reproduce photographs:*
A. A. Photo Library; All-Sport Photographic Ltd.; Austin
Rover Group Ltd.; Audi Volkswagen V.A.G. (U.K.) Ltd.;
Barratt Developments plc; Beken of Cowes Ltd.; BBC
Photographs; BBC Hulton Picture Library; British Library;
British Telecom; British Tourist Authority; Neill Bruce;
Camera Press Ltd.; Daily Telegraph Colour Library; Land
Rover Group; Mary Evans Picture Library; Fiat Auto (U.K.)
Ltd.; Colin Garratt; Ronald Grant Archive; Susan Griggs
Agency Ltd.; Image Bank; Interfoto Picture Library Ltd.;
Irish Tourist Board; Jaguar Cars Ltd.; Kobal Collection;
Littlewoods Pools Ltd.; Mansell Collection Ltd.; National
Motor Museum, Beaulieu; National Portrait Gallery; Network
Photographers; Nissan (U.K.) Ltd.; Photo Library
International; Plymouth Marketing Bureau; Pictorial Press
Ltd.; Pontin's Holidays; Popperfoto; Quadrant Picture
Library; Rex Features Ltd.; RoSPA; Rolls-Royce Motors Ltd.;
Saga Holidays plc; Philip K Sharpe/Oxford Scientific Films;
Spectrum Colour Library; Sporting Pictures (U.K.) Ltd.;
Syndication International; Volvo Concessionaires Ltd.;
Elizabeth Whiting & Associates; ZEFA Picture Library (U.K.) Ltd.;

and the following for their time and assistance:
Oxford Information Centre; Pickfords Travel; Randolph
Hotel, Oxford; Chit Chat Restaurant, Oxford; Debenhams
plc; Usbornes; Mota Market.

Studio and location photographs by:
Chris Honeywell, Rob Judges, Mark Mason, Terry Williams.

Illustrations by:
Alan Adler; Oena Armstrong; Judy Brown; Chris Burke;
Martina Farrow; Debi Gliori; Simon Gooch; John Ireland;
Mark Hackett; Andrew Harris; Gray Joliffe; Conny Jude;
Terry Kennett; Robert Kettell; Sally Lecky-Thompson;
Vanessa Luff; Kevin Lyles; Terry McKivragan; Willie Ryan;
Paul Sample; Kate Simpson; Michael Terry; Paul Thomas;
Christine Thwaites.

To the Student

We hope you are going to enjoy this book during your course and after it.

There are many different exercises in the book to help you learn not only the structures of English, but also when to use them. In each unit you will get a lot of practice in speaking and using the language in appropriate contexts.

Units 5, 10, 15 and 20 bring together the language of the previous units to give extra practice – and to give you a rest from learning new language!

In your Resource Book there are grammar reviews for each unit, extra exercises and also reading and listening passages. You can do all these at home; they will help you to remember what you have learned in the classroom. Don't forget to buy your copy of the Resource Cassette, too.

Enjoy your course!

Acknowledgements

We would like to thank everyone at the South Devon College of Arts and Technology, Torquay, especially Tom Hunter, Lorraine Davis, Linda Newton, Jerome Betts and Kath Green, and all the students who tried out the material in the early stages and offered valuable comments.

Thanks are also due to the staff and students at the College of St. Mark and St. John, Plymouth, for their encouragement and support.

Particular thanks to David Jolly, Jill Hadfield, Sue Mace and Jenny Pearson for letting us use their original ideas; and to Charles Hadfield, Tony Wright and Rachel Peterson for letting us use their poems and stories. The newspaper article on page 27 first appeared in the *Daily Mirror. Leaving on a Jet Plane* by John Denver is the copyright (1967) of Cherry Lane Music Publishing Co. Inc., and is used by permission.

A number of public bodies listened to and complied with our sometimes strange requests, including Torquay Police, Plymouth Tourist Information, and Plainmoor Swimming Pool, Torquay.

Thanks also to Mark Lowe, without whose initial encouragement this project would never have got off the ground; and to the staff at OUP – our editors Yvonne de Henseler and David Sawer, designer David Murray and art editor Saira Whitehead – who were more enthusiastic about the course than we were!

We are especially grateful to our Academic Mentors, Rod Bolitho and Chris Candlin, for their valuable advice and guidance.

Finally, thanks to those in our families who stayed with us and supported us to the bitter end, i.e. all the kids, present and future!

Val Black
Maggy McNorton
Angi Malderez
Sue Parker

1 >>> FIRST MEETINGS >>> 1

The Old way of Introduction. Published by Charles Tilt, 86, Fleet Street.   *The New way of Introduction.*

B Introductions

B1 😃 In the office canteen. Listen and study. What is the sales manager's name?

Informal

This is Rita. She's from Bonn.
Hello, Rita. Nice to meet you.
Hello.

Formal

Rita, I'd like you to meet Mr ....
How do you do?
How do you do?

B2 Introduce your partner to the people in the class. (Informal)

B3 Introduce your partner to the teacher. (Formal)

B4 Who is he/she? Where is he/she from?
Write about a person in the class (*not* your partner).
Ask your partner to show you this person.

_____

His/Her name ....

He/She ....   from ....

A Meeting someone new

A1 😃 Rita's first day at work. Listen and study.
Where is Rita from?

Hello, my name's John. What's your name?
Hello, I'm Rita. I'm from .... Where are you from?
I'm from Edinburgh.

A2 Tell your partner your name and where you are from. Ask him/her the questions in *A1*.

C Talking about interests and hobbies

C1 🔲 After work. Listen and study.
What is Rita interested in?

> What are you interested in?
>
> I'm interested in ....
>
> Do you like swimming?
>
> Yes, I do. What about you?
>
> No, I don't.

C2 Match the words with the pictures.

- [8] swimming
- [ ] sailing
- [ ] skiing
- [ ] dancing
- [ ] painting
- [ ] playing tennis
- [ ] taking photographs
- [ ] watching films

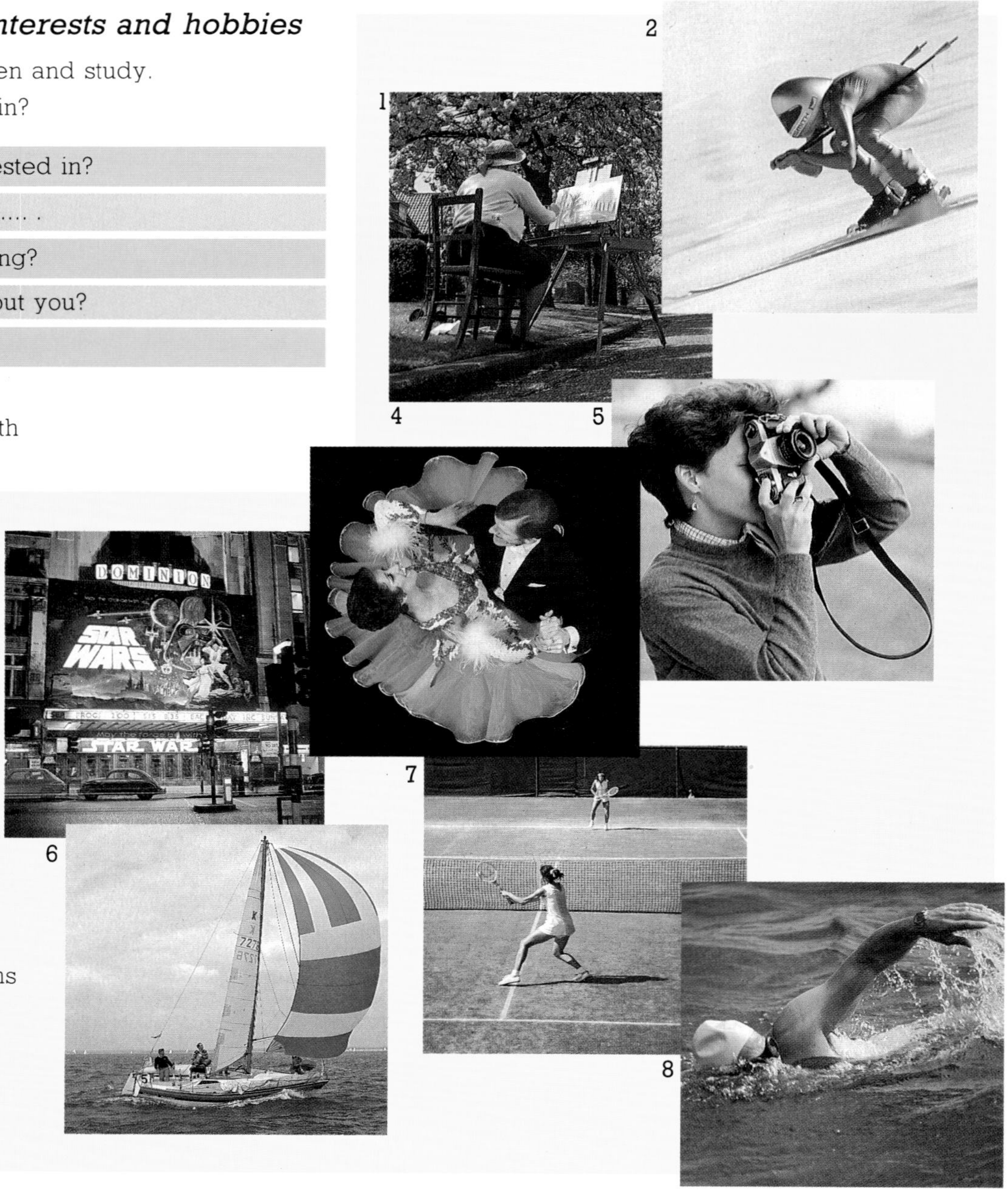

C3 Ask your partner about his/her hobbies.

C4 🔲 Listen and study.
What does Sally like doing?

> Does he like playing tennis?
>
> Yes, he does.
>
> Does she like swimming?
>
> No, she doesn't. But she likes ....

C5 Talk to another student and find out about his/her partner's hobbies.

C6 Ask other students about their hobbies, as in the example. Write them down.

A What are you interested in, Ahmed?
B Sailing.
A Do you like playing football?
B Yes, I do.

Student	Hobbies
Ahmed	Sailing, playing football

D Talking about families

D1 🔊 Listen and study.

How many boys has Rita got?

> Are you married?
>
> Yes, I am. And you?
>
> Yes, I've got a boy and a girl. Have you got any children?
>
> Yes, I have. I've got boys.
>
> Boys! How many have you got?
>
> .... !

D2 Complete this questionnaire. Ask your partner questions.

Example	You	Your partner
Have you got any brothers?		
Yes		
(How many brothers have you got?)		
2		
Have you got any sisters?		
No		
(How many sisters have you got?)		
—		
Are you married?		
Yes		
(Have you got any children?)		
Yes		
(How many children have you got?)		
3		
(Boys or girls?)		
2 boys, 1 girl		
......................................?		
......................................?		

D3 This is Suzanne's family. Match the words with the people in her family tree.

Suzanne

grandmother	2
son	
brother	
uncle	
cousin	
sister	
grandfather	
father	
cousin	
uncle	
aunt	
mother	
husband	
daughter	

Find the mothers-in-law!

D4 Ask your partner about his/her family. Try to draw his/her family tree.

E Jobs

E1 📼 Listen and study.

What is Alan's job?

> What do you do?
>
> I'm a .... How about you?
>
> I'm a secretary.
>
> Are you? Where do you work?
>
> I work in an office in the City.

E2 Ask your partner about his/her job.

E3 Match the jobs with the places.

1 FLORIST

2 DOCTOR

3 HAIRDRESSER

4 PHOTOGRAPHER

5 SECRETARY

6 LIBRARIAN

7 STUDENT

8 TEACHER

9 CHEF

10 CAR MECHANIC

8 SCHOOL	☐ COLLEGE
☐ SALON	☐ FLOWER SHOP
☐ GARAGE	☐ KITCHEN
☐ HOSPITAL	☐ OFFICE
☐ STUDIO	☐ LIBRARY

E4 What am I?

Work in small groups. Take turns.

1 Think of a job but don't tell the other students what it is.

2 Try to guess the job by asking questions like these:

DO YOU . . .

wear a uniform?	work . . . inside?
wear a suit?	outside?
wear overalls?	in the country?
make things?	in an office?
meet people?	in a bank?
travel?	on a farm?

Are you a ....?

E5 Interview about jobs

Complete this questionnaire. Write more questions.
Ask your partner the questions.

	Example	You	Partner
What do you do?	Teacher		
Where do you work?	School		
How many hours do you work?	35 hours		
When do you start work?	9.00 a.m.		
When do you finish work?	4.00 p.m.		
How do you travel to work?	Car		
How long does the journey take?	30 mins.		

E6 Tell the rest of the class about your partner's job.

E7 🔲 At a business meeting. Listen to these people introducing themselves, and complete the chart.

Name	Brian Gardner	Roberts	Bob	leveque
Home town	Bristol			
Age	39			
Married?	Yes			
Children	2			
Job	Computer programmer			
Interests	Travel			

A *Plymouth*

Plymouth is in the south-west of England, about 212 miles from London. It is one of Britain's most historic sea ports.

As you read the information about some of Plymouth's famous citizens, find the answers to these questions:

1 Two famous people from Plymouth did the same thing. What was it and who were they?
2 Write down the names of two boats.

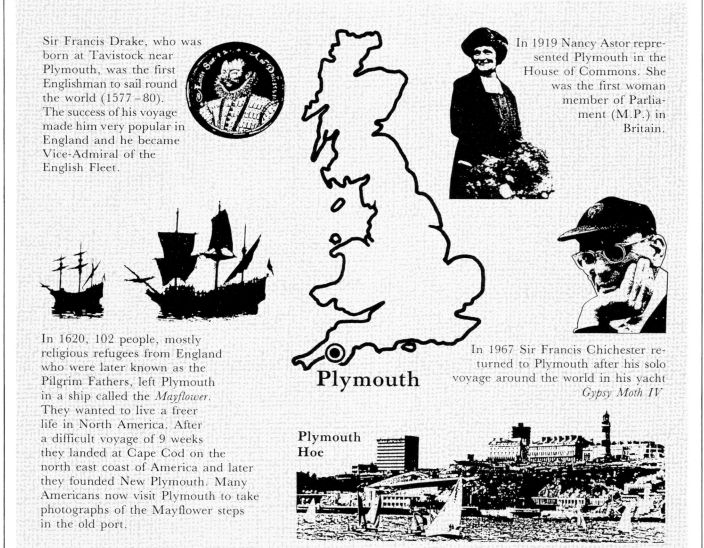

Sir Francis Drake, who was born at Tavistock near Plymouth, was the first Englishman to sail round the world (1577 – 80). The success of his voyage made him very popular in England and he became Vice-Admiral of the English Fleet.

In 1919 Nancy Astor represented Plymouth in the House of Commons. She was the first woman member of Parliament (M.P.) in Britain.

In 1620, 102 people, mostly religious refugees from England who were later known as the Pilgrim Fathers, left Plymouth in a ship called the *Mayflower*. They wanted to live a freer life in North America. After a difficult voyage of 9 weeks they landed at Cape Cod on the north east coast of America and later they founded New Plymouth. Many Americans now visit Plymouth to take photographs of the Mayflower steps in the old port.

Plymouth

In 1967 Sir Francis Chichester returned to Plymouth after his solo voyage around the world in his yacht *Gypsy Moth IV*

Plymouth Hoe

B Using a map

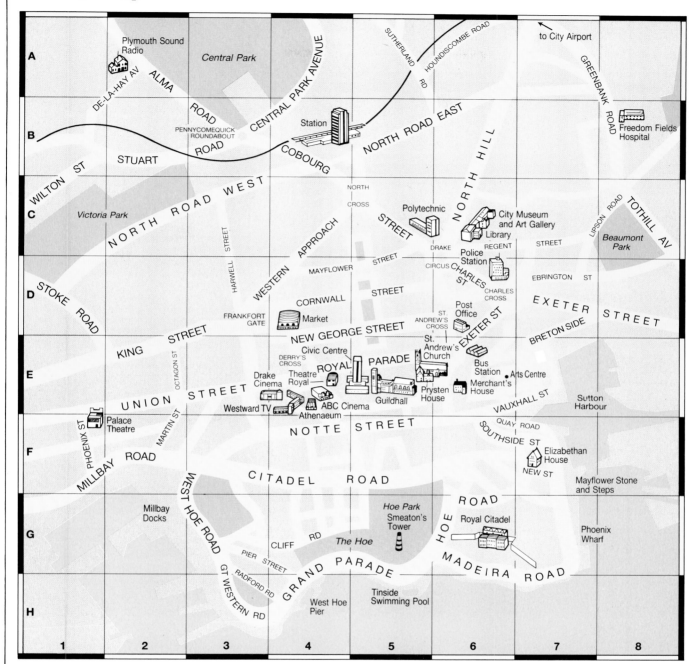

B1 Read and study. Find the places on the map.

The Library is next to the City Museum and Art Gallery. (C6)

The Athenaeum is between the ABC Cinema and Westward TV. (E4)

Tinside Swimming Pool is in front of Smeaton's Tower. (H5)

The Polytechnic is opposite the City Museum and Art Gallery. (C5)

The Police Station is near Charles Cross. (D6)

B2 Look at the map and complete the sentences. Use the same prepositions as in B1.

The Athenaeum is .... the ABC Cinema. (E4)

The Mayflower Steps are .... Phoenix Wharf. (F7)

Grand Parade is .... The Hoe. (G4-5)

The Market is .... Frankfort Gate. (D4)

The Civic Centre is .... the Theatre Royal and the Guildhall. (E5)

C Asking where places are

C1 🔊 Paolo Mazzetti is sight-seeing in Plymouth. Listen and study.

Where is the Guildhall?

> Excuse me, can you tell me where the Guildhall is, please?

> Certainly, it's .... St. Andrew's Church.

If you do not know the town, you can say:

> Sorry, I don't know. I'm a stranger here myself.

C2 Where are these places? Ask another student.

1 The Drake Cinema
2 The Market
3 The Merchant's House
4 The Elizabethan House
5 The Bus Station
6 The Theatre Royal

D Understanding directions

D1 Match the directions with the pictures.

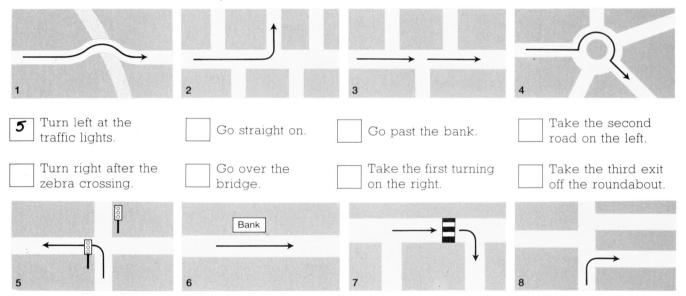

5 Turn left at the traffic lights.	☐ Go straight on. ☐ Go past the bank. ☐ Take the second road on the left.
☐ Turn right after the zebra crossing.	☐ Go over the bridge. ☐ Take the first turning on the right. ☐ Take the third exit off the roundabout.

D2 Give directions from A to B in these pictures.

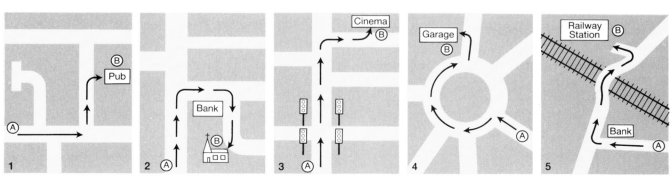

D3 🔈 Paolo is at the Civic Centre. Listen and study.

Mark Paolo's route to the Market on the map.

> Excuse me, can you tell me the way to the Market, please?

> Turn left.
> Go past the Theatre Royal to Derry's Cross.
> Take the first road on the right off Derry's Cross.
> Walk straight down until you come to another road. That's New George Street.
> The Market is directly opposite.

After giving directions, you can say this:

> You can't miss it!

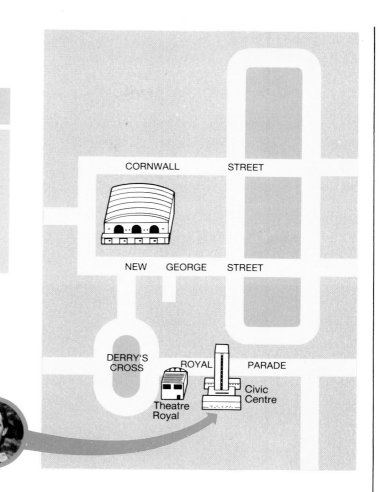

D4 🔈 Listen to these three people giving directions to places in Plymouth, starting from the Civic Centre. Follow the directions on the map of Plymouth, and write down the places.

The directions are to . . .

1 ....
2 ....
3 ....

D5 Directions game

1 Half the class are visitors to Plymouth.
2 Half the class live in Plymouth.
3 Take your maps of Plymouth and go round the class asking the way to different places.
4 If a visitor asks another 'visitor', don't forget that you can say, 'I'm sorry, I don't know. I'm a stranger here myself.'

D6 Imagine you live near the Library in Plymouth (C6 on the map). A friend is coming to visit you for the weekend. You give her directions from the railway station. Complete your note.

.... so when you get out of the station, turn ____ and then ____ ____ into Cobourg Street . Go over North Cross and ____ ____ Cobourg Street. When you come to Drake Circus ____ ____ into North Hill and the library is on your right. I live next door.

E Town facilities

E1 🔊 At the Tourist Information Centre. Listen and study.

Are there any good beaches in Plymouth?

> Is there a swimming pool in Plymouth?
>
> Yes, there is.
>
> Are there any good beaches?
>
> .... , ...
>
> Has Plymouth got a castle?
>
> No, it hasn't. But there are some fine old houses.

E2 The list below shows the town facilities in Plymouth. Ask your teacher about the facilities in the town you are in now. Ask your partner about his/her home town. Write in more places.

		Plymouth	Town you are in	Partner's home town
Transport	bus station	✓		
	railway station	✓		
	underground	✗		
	port	✓		
	airport	✓		
Sport/ Leisure	swimming pool	✓		
	football ground	✓		
	sports centre	✓		
	ice rink	✗		
	beaches	✓		
	parks	✓		
Cultural	theatre	✓		
	cinemas	✓		
	library	✓		
	art gallery	✓		
	museum	✓		

E3 The town you are in

Work in a small group. Find out:

1 The best place to eat.
2 The best place to have a drink.
3 What you can do in the evening.
4 The best things to see.
5 What you can see and do at the weekends.

3 ▶ SAYING WHAT YOU WANT ▶ 3

Requests | Permission | Restaurants and pubs | Telephoning

Gillie's Restaurant
MENU

STARTERS
Prawn cocktail
Cream of tomato soup
Pâté on toast
Fruit juices

MAIN DISHES
Fried fillet of plaice with lemon
Roast beef with Yorkshire pudding
Grilled gammon steak with pineapple
Our own traditional steak and kidney pudding

(all served with a selection of fresh vegetables)

DESSERTS
Apple pie with cream
Fresh fruit salad
Banana split

Coffee with cream

A What would you like?

A1 🎧 Listen and study.

What does the man want for his main course?

> What would you like, sir?

> I'd like prawn cocktail first.

> Very well, and for your main course?

> Could I have the .... ?

If you don't know what a dish is, you can say:

> Excuse me, what is Yorkshire pudding, exactly?

A2 What is it, exactly?

Ask the teacher if you don't know what these dishes are.

Steak and kidney pudding
Shepherd's pie
Cornish pasty
Welsh rarebit
Porridge
Irish stew

A3 You are in Gillie's Restaurant.

Work in small groups. Take turns to be the customers and the waiter or waitress.

Decide what you'd like. The 'waiter' or 'waitress' will come round for your order.

B Requests

B1 🔊 Listen and study.

> Could you bring the wine list, please?
>
> Certainly, sir.
>
> Would you bring me some bread, please?

B2 You and your partner are in the restaurant. Take turns to be the customer and the waiter or waitress. Ask him/her to do these things for you.

Can		get me some water,
Could	you	change this glass,
Would		turn the music down, please?
		....
		....

Certainly.
Sure.
OK/All right.
I suppose so.
Sorry, I'm afraid I can't. (+*reason*)

B3 Imagine you share a flat with someone. Write a note asking him/her to do some household jobs for you. Here are some ideas:

wash the dishes
tidy up
hoover the carpet
feed the cat
etc.

JACK,
I'VE GONE INTO TOWN TO DO THE SHOPPING. COULD YOU WASH THE DISHES, PLEASE? AND THE FLAT'S IN A TERRIBLE MESS........

C Permission

C1 🔊 Listen and study.

C2 Work in pairs. Take turns to be the guest and the landlady. Ask the landlady if you can do these things.

Can		have a bath,
Could	I	make some coffee,
May		use the telephone, please?
		....
		....

Certainly.
Sure.
OK/All right.
I suppose so.
I'm afraid you can't. (+*reason*)

C3 You want to give a party in your room tomorrow evening. Write a note to your landlady asking her permission. Here are some ideas:

borrow some glasses
use the kitchen to make sandwiches
take some furniture away
etc.

Dear Mrs White,
May I give a small party for a few friends in my room tomorrow evening? I haven't got many glasses, so......

D In the pub

D1 Read and study.

Pubs in England are normally open from 11.00 a.m. to 2.30 p.m. and from 5.30 p.m. to 10.30 or 11.00 p.m. Opening hours are even shorter on Sundays. Children under the age of 14 are not usually allowed in pubs; children under the age of 18 are not allowed to buy alcoholic drinks.

When a group of people go to the pub together, they usually buy drinks in 'rounds'. You order and collect drinks at the bar. We order beer and cider in *pints* or *half pints* (*halves*), wine in *glasses*, and spirits and other drinks *by name*.

THE UNDER 18 RULE

The law says that people Under 18 must not drink or purchase alcohol in this bar. The Licensee and Staff **will** refuse to serve alcohol to anyone who **is** - or **appears** to be - under 18.

D2 Continue these lists, using the drinks given.

A pint of bitter, please.

....

....

A glass of red wine, please.

....

....

A scotch, please.

....

....

mild	dry sherry
brandy	vodka and orange
dry white wine	Martini
lager	Guinness
rum and Coke	slimline tonic
lemon squash	shandy
sweet cider	Coke

D3 Listen and study.
What does Sue want to drink?

Would you like a drink, John?

Thank you, a half of bitter, please.

What would you like, Sue?

A glass of .... , please.

And what's yours, Rod?

Just a tonic, please.

Remember:

Thank you	=	Yes, please

D4 🔲 You are the barman/barlady. Listen to these three customers, make a note of their orders, and work out what they must pay.

```
                 PRICE LIST
Bitter           half  46p, pint 92p
Mild             half  47p, pint 94p
Lager            half  49p, pint 98p
Guinness         half  49p, pint 98p
Shandy           half  41p, pint 82p
Cider            half  43p, pint 86p
Bottled beer     47p
Wine             75p
Spirits          95p
Fruit juices, Coke  42p
Tonic            38p
```

Customer 1 must pay: £...
Customer 2 must pay: £...
Customer 3 must pay: £...

D5 It's your round

Work in small groups. Take turns to be the barman and the customer who orders the drinks. Ask what everyone would like and then go to the bar.

E Telephoning

E1 Read and study

	May I use your phone, please?	
It's	a local a long distance an international a reverse charge	call.

E2 Ask if you can use your landlady's phone for these calls.

1 to your family in your home town
2 to the school
3 to a friend on holiday in Scotland
4 to your embassy in London

E3 Telephone services

Use the Telephone Directory and/or the 'Telephone Dialling Codes' booklet for your area to complete this chart.

FIRE, POLICE, AMBULANCE	999
OPERATOR	....
DIRECTORY ENQUIRIES	....
TELEMESSAGES/TELEGRAMS	....
INTERNATIONAL OPERATOR	....
TIME CHECK	....
WEATHER FORECAST	....
WHAT'S ON	....

E4 International calls

Use the 'Telephone Dialling Codes' booklet to complete this chart.

	International prefix	Country code	Area code
Rome, Italy	010	39	6
Bonn, Germany (FDR)	010		
New York, USA	010		
Toulouse, France	010		
Luxembourg	010		
Your home town	010		

E5 Public telephones

These instructions for using public telephones are in the wrong order. Put them in the correct order.

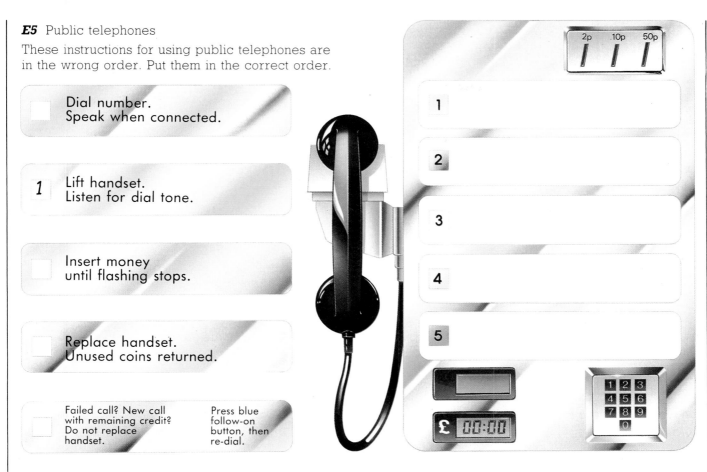

- [ ] Dial number.
  Speak when connected.

- [1] Lift handset.
  Listen for dial tone.

- [ ] Insert money until flashing stops.

- [ ] Replace handset.
  Unused coins returned.

- [ ] Failed call? New call with remaining credit? Do not replace handset. Press blue follow-on button, then re-dial.

E6 Answering the phone. Listen and study.

E7 Say these telephone numbers

37511   34967   43389   37724   74226   56609

>4 >> > WHAT'S THE MATTER? >> > 4

Advice and suggestions   *Making appointments*   *Health*

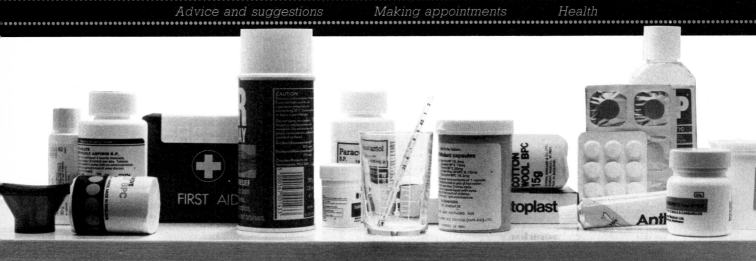

A Feeling ill

A1 🔲 Jill arrives at work feeling ill. Listen and study.

What's the matter with Jill?

| I'm not feeling very well. |
| Oh dear! What's the matter? |

| I've got a .... | Oh, I'm sorry. |

You can also say:

| I don't feel well. | What's wrong? |

And also:

| I feel awful. | What's the trouble? |

A2 Match the pictures with the words.

THE FIVE ACHES

1 backache
2 toothache
3 earache
4 stomach ache
5 headache

A3 Read and study.

| What's the matter? |

	foot	
My	finger	hurts.
	knee	
	arm	

or

	foot.
I've hurt my	finger.
	knee.
	arm.

Now talk to your partner about your health. Tell him/her about your aches. Tell him/her what hurts.

B Giving advice

B1 🔲 Listen and study.
What advice does the man give?

What can I do about it?
Well, why don't you take an .... ?
Yes, all right.

You can also say:

What about going to bed?
That's a good idea.

And also:

How about going to the doctor's?
Thanks. I'll do that.

B2 Tell your partner about one of the complaints. Your partner will give you suitable advice. Accept his/her advice.

I've got	a sore throat. a cut finger. a stomach upset. a rash. an insect bite. sunburn.

Why don't you	buy something for it at the chemist's? go to bed? go to the doctor's?

What about	buying something for it at the chemist's? going to bed? going to the doctor's?

What a good idea! That's a good idea. Thanks, I'll do that. Yes, all right.

C Rejecting advice

C1 Read and study.

If you don't want to take the advice, you can say:

No,	that's impossible. I'm afraid I can't do that. I don't think that's a good idea.

But you should also give a reason:

Pills make me feel sick.
I don't like staying in bed.
I haven't got time.

C2 You have got something wrong with you. Ask your teacher or your partner for advice. However, there is always a reason why you can't take the advice.

A What can I do about my .... ?
B Why don't you .... ?
A No, I can't do that. ....

D Who can help?

D1 Where do you go if you've got . . .
– a swollen finger?
– toothache?
– broken glasses?

D2 Read and study.

1 What is *your* situation in Britain?
2 What happens in your country about foreign visitors?

If you are ill while visiting Britain . . .

YOU DON'T PAY IF
1 you are from an EEC country
2 your country has a health agreement with Britain
3 you are on a course of study for 12 months or more

YOU DO PAY IF
you are from any other country, except in emergencies

YOU ALSO PAY FOR
1 medicines
2 glasses
3 dental treatment

E Making an appointment

E1 🔲 If you want a doctor, or a dentist, or an optician in Britain, you will have to make an appointment. Listen and study.

E2 🔲 Telephone the dentist for an appointment. Your words are printed below. The receptionist's words are on the tape. Read your words aloud and listen to the receptionist's replies. Fill in the appointment card.

Receptionist ....

You Hello, is that the dentist's?

Receptionist ....

You I'd like to make an appointment to see the dentist.

Receptionist ....

You No, not really. I need a check-up and two or three fillings.

Receptionist ....

You Right.

Receptionist ....

You Yes, that's fine.

Receptionist ....

You Yes, my name's.........

Receptionist ....

You It's spelled.........

Receptionist ....

You Friday is OK, but not in the morning, I'm afraid. Could I come in the afternoon?

Receptionist ....

You Yes, that's all right.

Receptionist ....

You Thanks very much. Goodbye.

APPOINTMENTS

NAME		
DAY	DATE	TIME

If you are unable to attend please advise immediately as a charge may be made for failure to keep appointments

F Suggestions

F1 🔲 You have learned some ways of giving advice or making suggestions. You can use them in other situations. Listen, read and study.

I'm bored. What can I do?

Why don't you watch TV?	Turn the radio on, then.
I can't, it's broken.	Yes, all right. But there's nothing good on.
Well, how about coming to the cinema with me, then?	Let's go to an art gallery, then.
There's nothing to see.	OK. If you pay for me.
In that case, what about going to a disco?	Why don't we go for a walk?
No, my feet hurt.	Good idea. Let's go!
I give up. You're impossible!	Right then!

F2 Everyone has a problem! Here are some examples.

I don't know what to give my brother for his birthday.

I can't find my coat.

I don't know where to go on holiday.

I can't do my homework.

I feel homesick.

I can't sleep.

In pairs, talk about your problems.

You	Your partner
State the problem →	
	Give advice
Accept or reject the advice ←	

S » FREEZE FRAME « S

A Finding out about people

PLAY BACK

Names	Unit 1,A
am/is/are	Unit 1,A
Telephone numbers	Unit 3,E
Ages	Unit 1,E

A1 A survey in the street. Listen and study. Fill the blanks.

What's your address?
15, ... Road.
How do you spell that?
W–I–N–D–S–O–R.
What's your telephone number?
Brighton ....

When's your birthday?
5th ....
How old are you? When were you born?
I'm .... I was born in ....

A2 Find out about the people in your class. Fill in the chart.

Name	Address	Tel. No.	Birthday	Year of birth

B People's daily routines

PLAY BACK

| Jobs | Unit 1,E |
| do/does | Unit 1,C |

B1 Read the article about Queen Elizabeth II. Find the answers to these questions.

1 How long does the Queen spend with Prince Philip?
2 What kinds of people does she meet?
3 Find three things that she does every day, and three things that she only does on this particular day.

Just another day in the life of...

A busy day for the Queen might go like this:

7 a.m. Wakes up, has a cup of tea. Reads The Sporting Life cover to cover.

7.30 a.m. Has a bath and gets dressed. The Queen selects her clothes but a personal maid lays them out in her dressing room.

8.00 a.m. Listens to BBC news and has breakfast with Prince Philip in the private Royal dining room. This usually consists of eggs or kippers, tea and toast. Both glance through all the newspapers as they eat. The Queen first opens The Times, then the Daily Telegraph, followed by the Daily Mirror.

8.45 a.m. Makes her daily phone call to the Queen Mother and Princess Margaret.

8.55 a.m. Sees Buckingham Palace housekeeper about domestic Palace matters.

9.10 a.m. Reads personal mail. Envelopes containing letters for the Queen's eyes only are marked with a special code.

9.30 a.m. First important business consultation with Private Secretary, Sir Philip Moore. The agenda is always heavy and the Queen has to make many decisions involving State and administrative matters.

10.15 a.m. Works on her daily State "boxes" which contain government documents.

11.00 a.m. Investiture in the Grand Ballroom of Buckingham Palace. The Queen remains standing and smiling for 90 minutes.

12.45 p.m. Quick lunch, often eaten alone in her private apartment – usually salad, fruit and mineral water.

1.30 p.m. Changes clothes for next engagement.

2.00 p.m. Leaves Palace to open hospital wing in Hertfordshire. Her route is always cleared by police.

3.00 p.m. Unveils plaque, makes speech, shakes dozens of hands at hospital. Cup of tea, eats nothing.

4.45 p.m. Back at the Palace and work in her office. Simply putting her signature to official papers can take 30 minutes.

5.30 p.m. Receives visiting foreign dignitary.

6.00 p.m. Final meeting of the day with her Private Secretary.

6.30 p.m. Quick change of clothes before leaving for a reception at St. James's Palace.

7.00 p.m. Arrives at St. James's Palace, shakes hand and talks to no fewer than 70 people.

8.15 p.m. Back at the Palace and changes into less formal clothes.

8.30 p.m. Informal dinner with Philip and a group of distinguished businessmen.

10.00 p.m. Watches television news.

10.15 p.m. Runs through the next day's engagements and finishes any official papers she has not yet had time to read.

10.30 p.m. Telephones some members of the Royal Family – just to see if all is well.

10.45 p.m. Bedtime. If Philip is ever out on an engagement alone, she always waits up for him before retiring.

11.15 p.m. Lights out.

B2 With your partner, ask and answer questions about the Queen's day.

What does she do	at 7? then? after that? next?	She has a cup of tea at 7 and reads a magazine. Then she . . . After that she . . . Next she . . .

B3 Compare the Queen's day with your day, and then with your partner's day.

	Queen	Me	Partner
7 a.m.	Wakes up, has cup of tea	Still asleep	
8.00 a.m.			
12.45 a.m.			
3 p.m.			
5.30 p.m.			
10.00 p.m.			

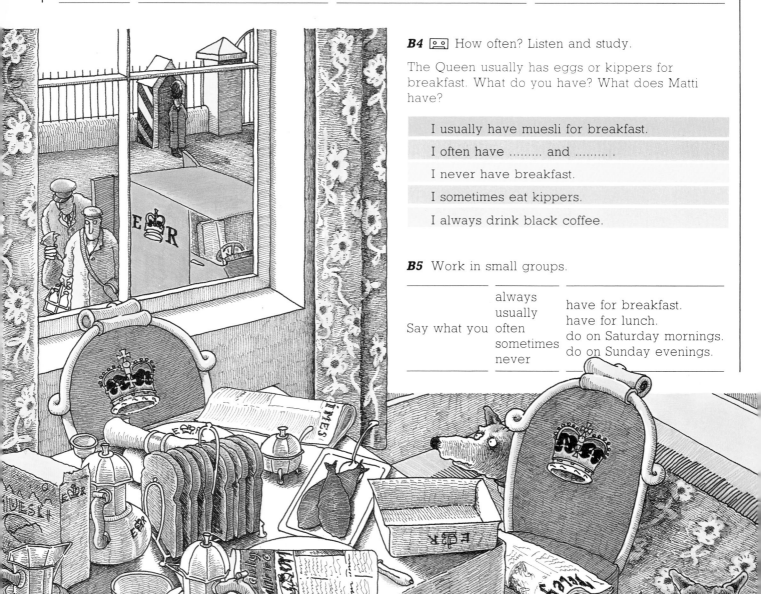

B4 How often? Listen and study.

The Queen usually has eggs or kippers for breakfast. What do you have? What does Matti have?

I usually have muesli for breakfast.

I often have .... and ....

I never have breakfast.

I sometimes eat kippers.

I always drink black coffee.

B5 Work in small groups.

Say what you	always usually often sometimes never	have for breakfast. have for lunch. do on Saturday mornings. do on Sunday evenings.

C People's habits

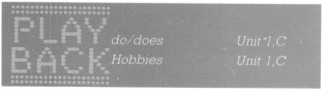

do/does Unit 1,C
Hobbies Unit 1,C

C1 You want a new flatmate. Is your ideal flatmate in the class? Find out by asking these and other questions. Put a tick (✔) in the right column. But first answer the questions yourself.

Do you . . .	Me always	Me usually	Me often	Me sometimes	Me never
get up early?					
smoke?					
sing in the bath?					
have noisy parties?					
do the washing up?					
put things away?					
go to bed late? etc . . .					

C2 Work in small groups. Talk about what sort of things annoy you when you live with someone.

C3 📼 Listen and study.

C4 Fill the blanks.

He's a dangerous driver.
He drives dangerously.

quick......*quickly*......

careful...........................

slow...............................

careless ....

bad.................................

He's a noisy eater.
He eats noisily.

angry ....

happy................................

He's a hard worker.
He works hard.

fast ....

He's a good singer.
He sings well.

C5 Answer these questions, and then ask three other people in the class.

		Me	1	2	3 ....
	eat?				
	dance?				
How do you	drive?				
	talk?				
	walk?				
	play tennis?				

well ANGRILY carefully easily beautifully sleepily carelessy sadly FAST QUICKLY Nervously NOISILY HAPPILY slowly BADLY

Now report back to the rest of the class, e.g.

Gina and Saif drive fast, but Selma drives slowly.

D The daily shopping

Directions	Unit 2, B-D
Saying what you want	Unit 3,A
has got/have got	Unit 1,D
some/any	Unit 2,E
Suggestions	Unit 4,F

D1 Match the shops with the things you can buy there.

D2 🎧 Listen and study.

How far is the chemist's?

> Is there a chemist's near here?
>
> Yes, go straight along South Street and it's on your left between the greengrocer's and the Post Office.
>
> How far is it?   About .... minutes' walk.

D3 You are outside the café in Castle Street. Ask your partner about other places.

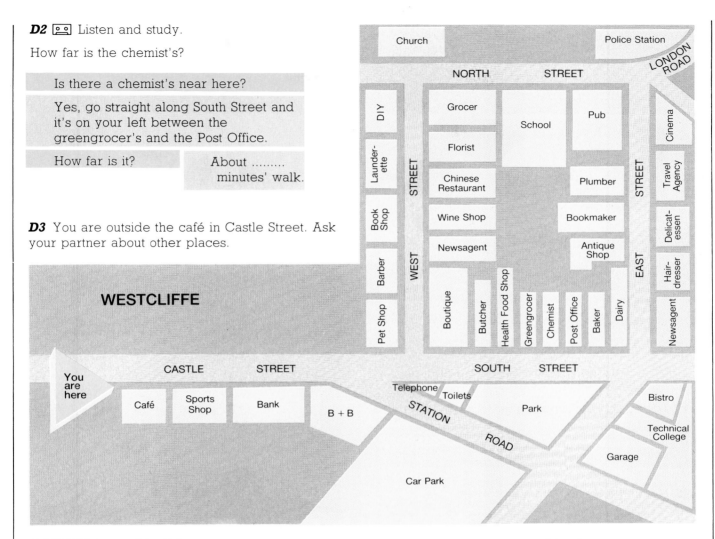

D4 🎧 Listen to this dialogue.

A Good morning. Can I help you?
B Good morning. Yes, I'd like some cheese, please.
A Yes, how much would you like?
B Er, half a pound, please.
A Anything else?
B Yes, have you got any free-range eggs?
A Yes, we have. They're fresh in today. How many do you want?
B A dozen, I think.
A Here you are. Anything else?
B Yes, could I have a pint of milk?
A I'm sorry, we haven't got any milk. Why don't you go to the dairy in South Street?
B OK. How much is that, please?
A That's 68p for the cheese and 96p for the eggs . . . that's £1.64, please.
B Here's two pounds.
A And here's your change, 36p. Thank you very much.
B Thank you, goodbye.

1 Write a list of six items of food.
2 This list is your shopping list. Go round the class and try to buy the items from other students. Use phrases from the dialogue.
3 The list is also what you have in your 'shop'. If a student asks for things on your list, sell them to him/her. If you haven't got them, suggest he/she goes to another shop in Westcliffe.

6 WHAT DOES HE LOOK LIKE? 6

Describing people   Faces and bodies   Clothes

A General appearance

A1 📼 Before the party. Listen and study.

What colour is Karl's hair? And his eyes?

> You know Karl . . .
>
> No, what does he look like?
>
> Well, he's tall and good-looking, with .... hair and .... eyes.
>
> Oh yes, I know who you mean. Let's invite him.

A2 Do these words describe men or women or both?

beautiful   **HANDSOME**

ATTRACTIVE   **pretty**

plain   **good-looking**

A3 Match the words with the pictures.

5	tall		short		medium height		fat/plump		thin/slim		average		well-built

A4 Work in pairs.

Student A	Student B
Draw the outline of a person. Make him/her short and fat, or tall and well-built. Your partner will ask you questions and try to draw the same outline. Answer only 'yes' or 'no'.	Try to draw the same outline as your partner, by asking questions like this: Is it a man? Is he/she tall? Don't look at your partner's drawing!

When you have finished, look at the drawings. Are they the same? Now exchange roles.

B Heads

B1 Read and study.

He's got short
brown hair.
He's got a
beard and a moustache.

She's got
long blonde hair.
She's got blue eyes and freckles.

He's bald,
and he wears glasses.

B2 Complete the sentences, using the words in the box. Use your dictionary to help you.

straight	snub	long	square	round
square	curly	pointed	long	wavy	hooked

 He's got .... hair, she's got .... hair, and I've got .... hair.

He's got a .... chin, and she's got a .... chin.

He's got a .... nose, she's got a .... nose, and he's got a .... nose.

He's got a .... face she's got a .... face, and I've got a .... face.

B3 Draw these things on the 'face'.

eyes
eyebrows
eyelashes
hair
moustache
beard
nose
ears
mouth
tongue
teeth
lips
cheeks
neck

B4 Put the words on the scales. (You may disagree!)

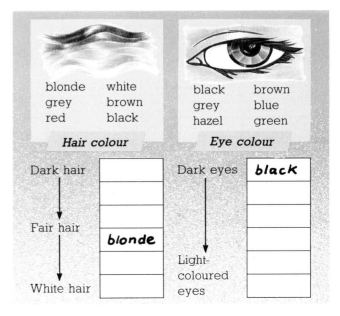

blonde	white
grey	brown
red	black

Hair colour

black	brown
grey	blue
hazel	green

Eye colour

Dark hair

Fair hair — *blonde*

White hair

Dark eyes — *black*

Light-coloured eyes

B5 📟 You are using an Identikit to form a picture of a wanted man.

Listen to the interview. Choose one from each of the five sets of features to form your picture.

If you're good at drawing, draw the face; if not, just put a ring round the correct letter.

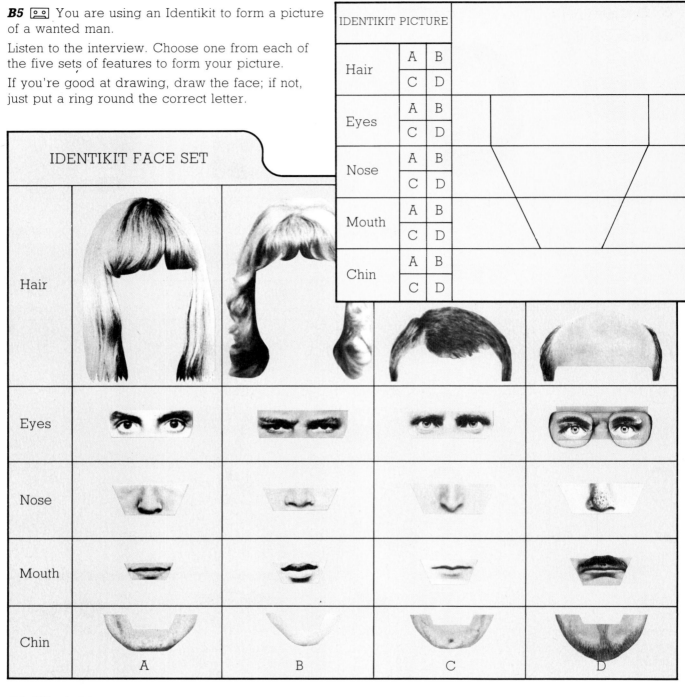

IDENTIKIT PICTURE			
Hair	A	B	
	C	D	
Eyes	A	B	
	C	D	
Nose	A	B	
	C	D	
Mouth	A	B	
	C	D	
Chin	A	B	
	C	D	

IDENTIKIT FACE SET

	A	B	C	D
Hair				
Eyes				
Nose				
Mouth				
Chin				

B6 Who is it?

Work in small groups. One person thinks of a member of the class. The rest of the group ask questions to guess who it is.

What shape is her nose?

What colour is her hair?

What colour eyes has she got?

How long is her hair?

B7 Remember that you can say:

She's attractive and slim, and she's got short blonde hair, a long nose and wide eyes.

or

She's attractive and slim, with short blonde hair, a long nose and wide eyes.

Write a description of someone in the class like the second description. Then read your description to your partner. Does he/she know who it is?

C The body and clothes

C1 Fill in the missing words.

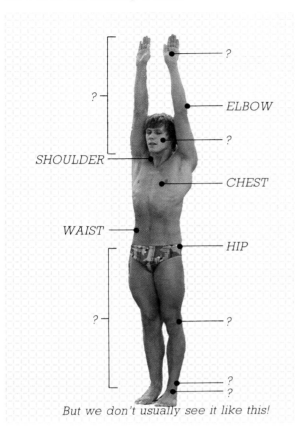

?
ELBOW
?
SHOULDER
CHEST
WAIST
HIP
?
?
?
?

But we don't usually see it like this!

C2 🔊 Listen and study.

What's he wearing?

He's wearing jeans and a blue sweater.

And what about Andrea?

She's wearing a pink dress and a white cardigan.

C3 Here are some more clothes. Put them into three lists – unisex, men's clothes and women's clothes. When you have finished, look at your lists – what do you notice about them? Which of the clothes are underwear?

C4 Back-to-back game

1 Look carefully at everyone in the class.
2 Stand back-to-back with a partner and ask questions, as in the example, about his/her clothes.
3 Move to another partner.

A Are you wearing brown cords?
B No, I'm not. I'm wearing green cords.
A Oh yes, and you're wearing a brown shirt.
B That's right.

D Missing person

D1 Read the poster.

Where can you see posters like this?
What should you do if you see this girl?

D2 Imagine you have to describe someone in the class for a police poster. Write the description.

WESSEX CONSTABULARY
MISSING PERSON
HAVE YOU SEEN THIS GIRL?

MARIA TERESA BERNINI
BORN 10.6.68 IN VERONA, ITALY.
WHITE, FEMALE, 1 metre 60
BROWN WAVY SHOULDER-LENGTH HAIR,
BROWN EYES, PROPORTIONATE BUILD

MARIA WAS LAST SEEN ON 7.8.85
WHEN SHE LEFT PARKSIDE HOTEL,
BOURNEMOUTH, ALLEGEDLY TO VISIT
SALISBURY PLAIN.

EXTENSIVE ENQUIRIES HAVE SO FAR
FAILED TO TRACE HER.

IF YOU HAVE ANY INFORMATION REGARDING HER WHEREABOUTS PLEASE CONTACT

THE INCIDENT ROOM AT RINGWOOD

TELEPHONE (0623) 729184 OR 813001
OR ANY POLICE OFFICER

7 WHICH DO YOU PREFER? 7

Experiences   Preferences   Comparisons   Places   Cars

A Experiences

A1 🔲 Looking at holiday brochures. Listen and study.

Which countries do the two women talk about?

> I'm thinking about my summer holiday.
> Have you ever been to .... ?

> Yes, I have. It's very beautiful.

> How about .... ? Have you ever been there?

> No, I haven't. I've never been to ....
> But I've been to ....

A2 Where have you been? Identify the places in the photographs and say if you have been there. Then ask your partner if he/she has been there. Then ask him/her about other holiday places he/she has been to.

I've been to . . .	I've never been to . . .
Have you ever been to . . . ?	Yes, I have/No, I haven't

A3 Ask four people in the class if they have ever done these things. Fill the chart.

Have you ever . . .	1	2	3	4
eaten porridge?				
drunk Guinness?				
flown in a Jumbo Jet?				
ridden in a Rolls-Royce?				
met a famous person?				
lived abroad for more than a year?				

A4 Report the results of your questions in *A3* to the rest of the class, e.g.

Abdul has eaten porridge, but the other three haven't.

B I prefer Portugal

B1 🔊 Listen and study.
Why does Avril prefer Portugal?

> Which do you prefer?

> I prefer Portugal to Algeria.

> Really? Why's that?

> Because it isn't quite so ....

> I think I'll go to Portugal, then.

B2 When you say you prefer one thing to another, you usually give a reason.

Because . . .	It isn't quite so hot.

Choose two countries and compare them. Say which you prefer and give reasons.

It's quieter.

the weather's better.

The people are more friendly.

It isn't so busy.

The food is better.

The beaches aren't so crowded.

There's more to do at night.

It's cheaper.

The countryside is more beautiful.

B3 🔊 In the school café. Listen and study.
Which does Rosa prefer?

> Do you prefer playing cards or reading?

> I prefer .... , because it's more relaxing.

> Me too.

> Well, I'd rather play cards because it's more fun.

B4 Ask two partners about the things they prefer. Ask about these things.
1 listening to pop music/classical music
2 living in the country/the town
3 reading romantic stories/detective stories
4 watching TV/listening to the radio
5 watching sport/playing sport

C Which is the best car?

C1 Read the advertisement about the new Audi 100. Use the words in the box to complete the sentences.

> the quietest
> noisier than
> not as quiet as

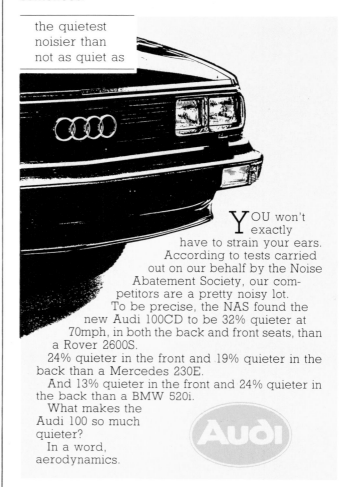

YOU won't exactly have to strain your ears. According to tests carried out on our behalf by the Noise Abatement Society, our competitors are a pretty noisy lot.
  To be precise, the NAS found the new Audi 100CD to be 32% quieter at 70mph, in both the back and front seats, than a Rover 2600S.
  24% quieter in the front and 19% quieter in the back than a Mercedes 230E.
  And 13% quieter in the front and 24% quieter in the back than a BMW 520i.
  What makes the Audi 100 so much quieter?
  In a word, aerodynamics.

A Rover 2600 is .... the new Audi 100.
The Mercedes 230E is .... the new Audi 100.
The Audi 100 is .... of the four cars in the test.

C2 🔊 In the pub. Listen and study.
Which car does the second man prefer?

> I think the Rolls-Royce is the best car in the world.

> I don't think so. A .... is much better.

> Well, the Rolls-Royce is more comfortable than any other car.

> But it isn't as stylish as the ....

Cadillac

Fiat Uno

Range Rover

Volvo Estate

Citroën 2CV

Metro

VW Polo

Nissan Cherry

Jaguar

Lamborghini

Rolls-Royce

C3 Discuss the cars in the photographs.

noisy/quiet
slow/fast
big/small
long/short
wide/narrow
good/bad

stylish/plain
expensive/cheap
economical/
   uneconomical
comfortable/
   uncomfortable

D The Road to Wigan Pier

D1 In 1937 George Orwell, an English writer and socialist, wrote a book called *The Road to Wigan Pier* about the lives of working people in an industrial town in the north of England.

In 1983 a reporter from *The Sunday Times* newspaper revisited Wigan to see if life for working people had changed.

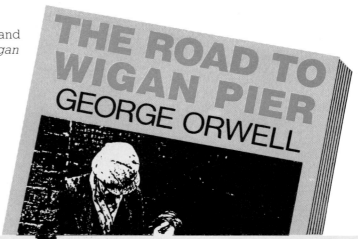

• In 1937 . . . •

In 1937, Orwell found a family – father unemployed, two small children – who were living on £1.60 a week from the dole. Orwell itemised the family's budget, and the comparison with today is interesting. First Orwell's list, converted from shillings and pence:

Rent	45p	Milk	4p
Clothing Club	15p	Union fees	1p
Coal	10p	Insurance	1p
Gas	7p	Food	77p
		Total	£1.60

• In 1983 . . . •

The weekly budget of today's unemployed family of four, the Armitages in Marsh Green, from a total income of £73.60:

Rent	£20
Coal	£10
Electricity	£4
TV (a slot meter – 50p for six hours)	£4
TV licence stamp	£1
Telephone	£2
Interest and repayment on £400 loan for washing machine	£7.50
HP on husband's suit and shoes	£2
Food	£18
Total	£68.50

D2 Compare the budgets of the two families. To help you, here are the percentages of the total budget spent on separate items.

% of total	1937	1983
Rent	28%	29%
Fuel	11%	20%
Food	51%	26%
Other	10%	25%

What is the biggest difference between life in 1937 and 1983?

Is life better now than it was?

D3 Orwell's book and *The Sunday Times* article are about unemployment. In 1985 there were at least 3½ million people unemployed in Britain, or about 12% of the workforce.

How many people are unemployed in your country? What percentage of the workforce is it?

What problems do unemployed people face?

What solutions does the government in your country offer to the unemployed?

8 >> SAY WHAT YOU THINK! >> 8

Opinions   Agreeing   Disagreeing   Personal tastes   Social problems

Do you like my new hat?

I'm afraid I don't, really. I think it's a bit old-fashioned.

Well, it's not bad.

Yes, I do. I think it's lovely.

A Do you like my . . .

A1 Listen and study.

A2 Make conversations with your partner about the things in the photographs.

Do you like my . . . ?

Yes, I think it's/they're . . .

Well, it's/they're . . .

I'm afraid I don't. I think it's/they're . . .

very friendly

very nice

pretty

lovely

beautiful   wonderful

rather unfriendly

rather noisy

a bit old-fashioned

too old

all right

B Personal tastes

B1 Look at the chart. Put a ring round the things you like and cross through the things you don't like.

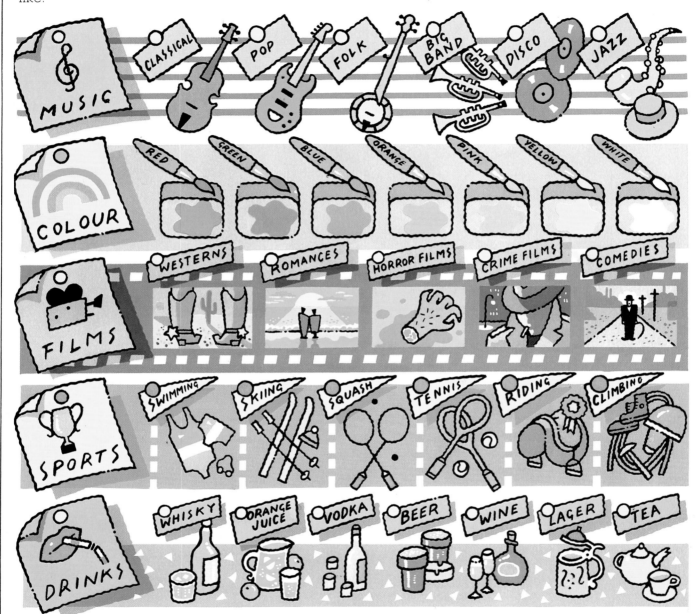

B2 🔊 In the school café. Listen and study.

| I like classical music. |
| So do I. |
| Do you? *I don't.* |

B3 Work in pairs. Discuss the things in the chart that you like. Do you like the same things?

B4 🔊 Listen and study.

| I don't like disco music. |
| Neither do I. |
| Don't you? *I do.* |

B5 Now discuss with a new partner the things you don't like in the chart. Do you dislike the same things?

C All things British

C1 🎧 What do you think of Britain? Listen and study.

> What do you think of the British?
>
> I think they're crazy.
>
> Yes, I think so, too.   Really? *I* don't.

> What do you think of British beer?
>
> I don't think it's very good.
>
> I don't think so, either.   Really? *I* do.

C2 Here are two opinions of Britain and the British. Which opinions do you agree with? Say why.

'I think the British are crazy. They drive on the wrong side of the road, have cold bedrooms and eat fish and chips all the time. I don't think much of British beer and British food is tasteless . . .'.

'I think the British are fantastic. They're always very friendly and helpful to strangers. British food isn't bad, either. Roast beef and Yorkshire pudding is my favourite dish and I always enjoy the desserts . . .'

C3 Say what you think of these things and give reasons.

1 British weather
2 Big cities
3 Pets
4 Pop music
5 Women drivers
6 Football

A I think British pubs are great.
B Why's that?
A Because the atmosphere's so good.

D Facts and opinions

D1 Give your opinions about these facts.

1 Children aren't allowed in pubs.
2 There are no waiters or waitresses in pubs.
3 Pubs don't usually sell tea or coffee.
4 English beer isn't always cold.

FACTS
Pubs in England aren't open all day.
Pubs in England close at 10.30 or 11 p.m.

OPINIONS
Pubs should be open all day.
Pubs shouldn't close so early.

D2 Listen and study.

Do you think pubs should be open all day?			Pubs shouldn't close so early.		
Yes, I do.	No, I don't.	I don't know.	I agree.	I disagree.	I don't think it matters.

D3 Ask the people in the class for their opinions about the facts in D1.

D4 Opinions questionnaire

Do you agree or disagree with these opinions? Fill the chart. Then interview your partner. What does he/she think?

	Agree	Disagree	Don't know	Not important
A Old people				
1 Old people should live with their sons and daughters.				
2 Old people should have more money.				
3 People should retire at 55.				
B Children				
4 Children shouldn't eat sweets.				
5 Children should go to bed early.				
6 Children should start school when they are 5.				
C Parents				
7 Parents shouldn't hit their children at all.				
8 Parents should know everything about their children.				
9 Parents should give their children everything they want.				
D Young people				
10 Young men should do military service.				
11 Young women should do military service.				
12 Young people should leave home at 18.				
E Crime				
13 Murderers should be hanged.				
14 Drivers shouldn't drink and drive.				
15 Policemen should carry guns.				

E Community Centre

Some people have nowhere to go in their free
time. One solution to the problem of leisure is a
Community Centre where young and old people
can go to meet their friends. The Centre can have
a lot of different activities.

You are redeveloping an old factory as a
Community Centre in the town where you live.
Look at the plan of the building below.

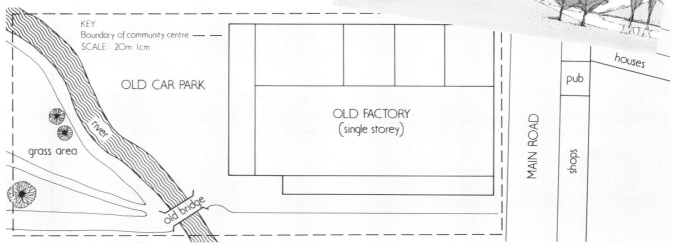

Work in groups. Organize a meeting in your group
to discuss what the Centre should have so that
everybody can go there; use the Agenda below.
Write down your decisions in the Minutes. Then
report to the other groups.

AGENDA

1 When should the Centre be open?

2 How many people should work there?

3 What sports should there be in the
Centre?

4 Should there be any educational
classes?
Which ones?

5 Should there be a café? A bar? A
restaurant?

6 What other activities should there
be?

7 How much should people pay to use
the Centre?

Use language like this:

I think | we should . . .
there should be . . .
it should have . . .

Yes, I think so too./Yes, I agree.

No, I don't think so./No, I disagree.

MINUTES
1 Times –
2 Workers–

A Are you free tonight?

A1 ☐ Listen and study.

A2 Remember:

Today	Tomorrow	Friday
this morning	tomorrow morning	on Friday morning
this afternoon	tomorrow afternoon	on Friday afternoon
this evening	tomorrow evening	on Friday evening
tonight	tomorrow night	on Friday night

A3 Maggy is a part-time teacher, a mother and a housewife. This is her diary for the week. Her friend Val wants to play tennis with her.

In pairs, take turns to be Maggy and Val. Ask if Maggy is free at these times:

Monday morning	Friday morning
Monday afternoon	Friday evening
Tuesday evening	Saturday afternoon
Wednesday morning	Saturday evening
Thursday afternoon	

> Are you free on Monday morning?
>
> No, I'm not. I'm teaching.

A4 In groups, talk about your arrangements for this week.

Week Planner

MON.
9–1pm. School
6pm Children→ Swimming

TUES.
10.30am. Take Mark→ Dentist
1–4pm. School

WED.
9–1pm School
PREPARE LESSONS!

THUR.
9–1pm. School
2pm. Hairdresser's

FRI.
1–4pm. School
8pm. Dinner with John

SAT.
10am. Yoga
2pm Children→riding

SUN.
1pm. Lunch with Mother

B Inviting

B1 Read and study.

> Would you like to go to the cinema with me tonight?

> Sorry,   I'm afraid I can't.
>   I'm playing tennis.
>   I don't like the cinema.

or

> Yes,   I'd love to!
>   that would be nice.
>   all right.

B2 In pairs, take turns to invite each other to do these things. Answer truthfully!

go to the cinema
go to the beach
go to a club
go to a disco
go out for a meal
go out for a drink
go out for a walk
come to lunch
come to dinner
come to my house

B3 This is your diary for the week. Find someone in the class to do these things with you:

go for a walk   go to a disco
go to a concert   spend a quiet evening at
go to the cinema   home
have dinner   play tennis

Fill your diary. But you must not do the same thing twice in the week. And you must not see the same person twice in the week.

Week Planner

MON.	THUR.
TUES.	FRI.
WED.	SAT.
	SUN.

C What are you going to do?

C1 🔊 In the school café. Listen and study.
What is Rosa going to do?

> What are you going to do after the course?

> I'm going to .... a bit. What are you going to do?

> I'm going to look for another job.

C2 What are your plans for the future?
What are you going to do . . .

– this weekend?
– during the course?
– next week?
– after the course?
– when you go home?

D Entertainments

D1 Saturday evening at home. Listen and study.

What do the four people want to do?

> I'd love to see .... I love plays.

> I don't. I like the cinema. I'd like to see ....

> I don't mind the cinema, but I prefer television. I wouldn't mind watching the ....

> Well, I can't stand TV. I'd rather go to a ....

1

DUSTIN HOFFMAN
Tootsie
1983 Columbia Pictures Industries, Inc.
Sep Progs Sun to Thur: 2.35, 5.55, 8.40
Fri & Sat: 2.35, 6.55, 9.40

2 Michael Caine, Julie Walters
Educating RITA 15
Sep Progs Sun to Thur: 2.05, 5.35, 8.15
Fri & Sat: 2.05, 6.35, 9.15

3 Burt Lancaster
LOCAL HERO PG
Sep Progs Sun to Thur: 2.00, 5.55, 8.25
Fri & Sat: 2.00, 6.55, 9.25

4 DARIO ARGENTO
TENEBRAE 18
...TERROR BEYOND BELIEF
Sep Progs Sun to Thur: 2.25, 5.30, 8.45
Fri & Sat: 2.25, 6.30, 9.45

TV

EVENING VIEWING

10.0 News at Ten
followed by
Thames News Headlines

10.30
Hill Street Blues
DANIEL J TRAVANTI
EUGENE'S COMEDY
EMPIRE STRIKES BACK

Folk
JACKSON'S LANE COMMUNITY CENTRE, Archway Road, Highgate: Stoned Dates, Wednesday at 8.30 p.m.
ARCHWAY TAVERN, Archway Roundabout: Irish Mist tonight (Thursday) at 9 p.m. Free.
COCK TAVERN FOLK CLUB, 27 Great Portland Street, Regent's Park: Martin Simpson tonight (Thursday) at 8 p.m. £2 plus concs.

11.30 Edgar Wallace Presents
ANN FIRBANK
JOHN THAW
DEAD MAN'S CHEST
FILM David Jones and Johnnie Gordon, two young, impoverished and cynical journalists, plan a fake murder. But the scheme goes wrong. Made in black and white.
See page 19
Mildred   Ann Firbank
David   John Thaw

THE SCHOOL FOR SCANDAL

D2 Read and study.

	General		Particular		
100%	I love I like I don't mind I don't like I hate	plays.	I'd love I'd like I don't want I'd hate	to see	*The School for Scandal.*
0%	I can't stand		Remember also: I wouldn't mind seeing *The School for Scandal.*		

D3 In groups, discuss what you would like to do together on Saturday evening. Use the advertisements above, or look at the Entertainments Page in the local newspaper.

E Newspapers

E1 In Britain there are two kinds of newspapers: national and local. A local newspaper usually has a small circulation whereas national newspapers can sell up to 4 or 5 million copies a day. Local newspapers are often read only in one town, city or county, but national newspapers are read all over the country.

There are two kinds of national papers: 'popular' and 'quality'. The *Sun*, the *Star*, and the *Daily Mirror* are examples of popular papers. The *Guardian*, the *Daily Telegraph* and *The Times* are quality papers.

You can buy newspapers at a newsagent's, 'daily' papers during the week, and on Sunday, quality papers such as the *Observer* and *The Sunday Times*, and popular papers such as the *News of the World*.

E2 Look quickly at the newspaper page on the next page.

1 What is the name of the paper?
2 What date was it printed?
3 How much did it cost?
4 What is the main headline?
5 Who are the men in the photographs?
6 What was the weather forecast for Coronation Day?
7 What is the advertisement for?
8 What is the man in the cartoon holding?
9 Where can you find a description of the Queen's dress?

49

NEWS CHRONICLE

No. 33,381   TUESDAY, JUNE 2, 1953   PRICE 1½d.

49

THE CROWNING GLORY
EVEREST IS CLIMBED

49
THE QUEEN'S DRESS TODAY *Back Page*

Tremendous news for the Queen

HILLARY DOES IT

GLORIOUS *Coronation Day news! Everest—Everest the unconquerable—has been conquered. And conquered by men of British blood and breed.*

The news came late last night that Edmund Hillary and the Sherpa guide, Bhotia Tensing, of Colonel John Hunt's expedition, had climbed to the summit of Earth's highest peak, 29,002 feet high.

New Zealand's deputy premier announced it at a Coronation Day ceremony at Wellington —and within seconds it flashed round the world.

Queen Elizabeth the Second, resting on the eve of her crowning, was immediately told that this brightest jewel of courage and endurance had been added to the Crown of British endeavour. It is understood that a message of royal congratulation is being sent to the climbers.

Hillary, a 34-year-old New Zealander, and Bhotia Tensing, 38-year-old leader of the guides and bearers, are said to have made the final 1,000-foot ascent from Camp Eight on the upper slopes.

The feat was apparently accomplished on Monday.

A year ago Bhotia Tensing climbed to within 800 feet of the summit with Raymond Lambert, in the unsuccessful Swiss attempt.

NEWS BY RUNNER

The latest news of the progress of the expedition hitherto—despatched by runner and received in London yesterday—was that the climbers were ready, as soon as the weather was suitable, to set out from Camp Seven, established high on the South Col at about 26,000 feet, to pitch Camp Eight high up near the summit. Events have overtaken the runners.

David Walker here reconstructs from the known methods of Everest climbing how the final assault is likely to have been achieved.

The two figures are in wind-proof smocks of different colours, double-lined with nylon, and each wears two hoods. Beneath the visors the eyes peer out on the roof of the world from goggles greased against frosting.

Down to the right lies Tibet and to the left Nepal, while death in a variety of forms, none pleasant, lurks on every side.

At such a height no man can survive without extra oxygen, involving 26lb. of dead weight, when every ounce can count; but at this stage science must supply what nature will not give. The endurance-time of this oxygen, carried in the back cylinders, is estimated at five hours.

Hands are lumpy in three sets of gloves: outer gauntlets of windproof cotton enclose mittens made of down. Next to the skin, worn tight, are gloves of silk.

It may be necessary for one or other of the men to look at his watch. This is a major decision because of the intense effort of will that must be followed by the physical distraction. It can take a minute to carry out.

TEN STEPS A MINUTE

Step by step, in Martian clothing, the two figures move forward, pursuing their race against time and the mountain in the slowest of slow motion. Ten steps a minute, Eric Shipton tells me, could be considered satisfactory; five hundred feet an hour is what their leader, Colonel Hunt, was hoping for. The estimates roughly tally.

The boots used for so many weeks in the early stages have been discarded. The pairs now worn are not even waterproof.

Turn Page Two, Col. 3

49
The new Elizabethan

EDMUND HILLARY, whose conquest of Everest sets the seal on the new Elizabethan age, is a 34-year-old bee farmer from New Zealand.

He learned his mountaineering in the Alps of the little Dominion of two million people, and was a pioneer in introducing winter ski-ing there.

He and George Lowe, the other New Zealander of the party, were making a free-lance climb in the Himalayas when Eric Shipton's "look - see" expedition arrived in 1951 to choose a route up Everest. Hillary and Lowe dropped their own project and trailed halfway across the vast range to join them.

Told of Hillary's achievement, New Zealand's Prime Minister, Mr. Sidney Holland, said: "What a grand achievement on the eve of the Coronation! I hope this terrific example of tenacity, endurance and fortitude in this our Coronation year may be regarded as a symbol that there are no heights or difficulties which the British people cannot overcome."

SMILING, mountain - wise Bhotia Tensing, is the leader of the Sherpa guides and porters who accompanied the expedition.

He is 38 and a veteran of four previous attempts on Everest by the northern route. His Sherpa comrades call him the Tiger.

On May 28 last year Tensing climbed to 28,215 feet with Raymond Lambert of the unsuccessful Swiss expedition before the failure of their oxygen apparatus forced them back.

Tensing's people are a caste of mountain dwellers whose "capital" is Namche Bazar, on the road to Everest. They live by trading with Tibet, Nepal and India.

Prophet Vicky

Yesterday's cartoon from Vicky on holiday.

Malenkov going to the ball

Moscow, Monday. — Mr. Malenkov, Russian Prime Minister, will go to a Coronation Ball at the British Embassy in Moscow tomorrow night. With him will be Mr. Molotov, Foreign Minister, and 200 senior officials.

49
Here the forecast is rain—hail—sun—storm, BUT the crowds are singing in the rain SO—

WHO CARES NOW IF IT SNOWS?

CORONATION DAY FORECAST : Northerly winds, sunny spells, showers with hail and thunder, cold. Mid-day temperature 55 deg.

NEWS CHRONICLE REPORTERS

REPEATED heavy showers lashed the packed campers lining the Royal Way last night. Then the sky cleared and the temperature dropped 13 degrees in a few hours.

But the campers sat it out. And early this morning, cut by a chill wind under the stars, they could still raise a cheer for Britain's Everest victory.

When the news spread, people started shouting : "The new Elizabethans!" Hundreds woke from their blanket beds to dance and sing.

By 1 a.m. 50,000 people were squatting in The Mall. Another 50,000 were camped in Trafalgar Square. Along the route stretched the queue—at a temperature of 45 degrees.

And still they came—from early morning trains at main-line stations, and from 18,000 cars converging on London every hour.

FIRES LIT IN STREETS

People already on the pavements lit fires to keep warm, cooked snacks and tea on spirit stoves, played cards, sang—or tried to sleep.

Earlier, thousands of cheering people surrounded the Queen Mother and Princess Margaret as they drove from Buckingham Palace after spending two hours with the Queen in her private apartments—a last visit before the Coronation.

Reinforced police could not clear a way : the car was halted for 15 minutes beside the Victoria Memorial.

The Queen Mother, in a white feathered gown and off-the-face white hat, and Princess Margaret, in a low-cut smoke-blue gown, waved. Motor-cycle police came to the rescue. But a little later more crowds ran from their pitches and blocked the route to Clarence House.

Fifty thousand people gathered outside Buckingham Palace. Despite the bitter wind, they danced away the hours, sang hymns and popular songs and for hour after hour chanted : "We want the Queen ! "

Once the curtains parted above the Palace balcony and a roar went up.

Scotsmen sang "On the bonnie, bonnie banks of Loch Lomond." An elderly man wearing a black homburg hat and carrying a silver-topped cane led hundreds in The Big Apple.

JEWEL GUARD

Outside Westminster Abbey the carpenters, painters and carpet-layers were putting the finishing touches. Six men trimmed and nailed down the plush-blue carpet on which the Queen will step from her coach. Another daubed the last touch of yellow to the Abbey annexe. Two hundred and fifty of them have worked there. Twelve have Coronation seats.

Inside was the Coronation regalia brought earlier in the day from the offices of the Goldsmiths and Silversmiths Company in Regent Street, where it had been prepared for today's ceremony.

The priceless jewels—including St. Edward's Crown and the Imperial State Crown—were laid out on tables in the Jerusalem Chamber, guarded by yeoman warders.

Pictures ; Page Five

49
Stabbed girl dead in Thames

News Chronicle Reporter

A MURDERED girl was found in the Thames yesterday ; and last night the police feared her girl companion had been killed too.

The girl in the river was 16-year-old Barbara Songhurst, a chemist's assistant, of Princess Road, Teddington. She was stabbed three times in the back after being assaulted on Lovers' Towpath at Ham, Surrey.

On Sunday Barbara went cycling with her friend, 18-year-old Christina Reed, of Roy Crescent, Hampton Hill.

See Page Five

Flash kills 3 cricketers

Lightning struck three cricketers dead at a Coronation match yesterday The flash shot through the dressing room at a soap factory's ground at Irlam, near Manchester.

The men killed were Ernest Taylor, 44, Herbert Vaudrey, 37, and George Perry, 31, all of Cadishead.

CENTRAL 5000

WEATHER — Showers and short sunny intervals. Midday temp 50-55. Sun rises 4.45 a.m., sets 9.10 p.m. Moon 06.35 a.m.-9.34 a.m. Lights 10.07 p.m.-3.49 a.m. tomorrow High water at London Bridge 5.48 a.m.-5.54 p.m.

Weather map, Page Two

49
REST OF THE NEWS

ONE of the greatest footballers of the century, Alex James, died in a London hospital yesterday.

A little man, he always wore long, baggy shorts. The crowd loved that as well as his play. *Alex, by Bernard Joy: Page Five*

Rhee's price

SYNGMAN RHEE, President of South Korea, has stated his terms for accepting United Nations truce terms He wants a mutual defence pact with America.—*See Page Two.*

Pinza favourite

PINZA, Gordon Richards's mount, has overtaken the Queen's colt Aureole as favourite for the Derby. He was 5 to 1 at last night's call-over.— *Captain Heath; Page Nine.*

In other pages—

T V comes into its own—Page Three.
The Mighty Paradox That Works—Page Four.
Orange box stand for Prince Charles—Page Five.
It's a Family Affair—Page Six.
The Route, The Times—Page Seven.
In The Abbey and London—after-dark guide—Page Eight.

"A SMITHS CLOCK my dear, is the Unforgettable Gift for Coronation Year"

Here is indeed a gift that will be a constant link for years and years to come with this outstanding period in our history. Whether it is for a wedding or a birthday, or a reminder for those 'back home' that British Craftsmanship is still the best . . . give Smiths Clocks in Coronation Year!

Sold in a great variety of beautiful models by leading Jewellers everywhere.

Models from 19/-

ROPER
Handsome Walnut or Mahogany case 8 day clock with bigar and half-hour strike on coiled gong. Strikes. Series. 68.12.6. Clocks. £13.5.0.

SMITHS ENGLISH CLOCKS LTD., LONDON N.W.2
The Clock and Watch Division of S. Smith & Sons (England) Ltd.

10 ≫ FREEZE FRAME ≪ 10

A Sport

Describing people	Unit 6,A-C
Experiences	Unit 7,A
Preferences	Unit 7,B
Comparisons	Unit 7,B-C
Likes and dislikes	Unit 8,A-B
Opinions	Unit 8,C-D

A1 Sort it out!

Match the sport and the equipment with the picture.

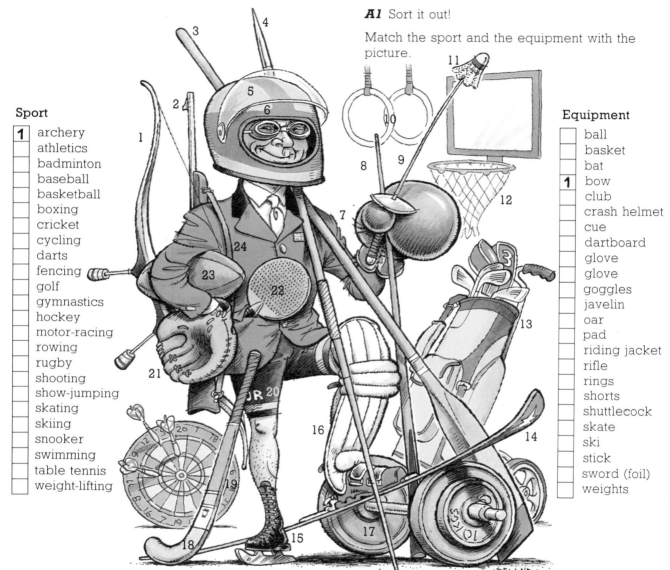

Sport

1	archery
	athletics
	badminton
	baseball
	basketball
	boxing
	cricket
	cycling
	darts
	fencing
	golf
	gymnastics
	hockey
	motor-racing
	rowing
	rugby
	shooting
	show-jumping
	skating
	skiing
	snooker
	swimming
	table tennis
	weight-lifting

Equipment

	ball
	basket
	bat
1	bow
	club
	crash helmet
	cue
	dartboard
	glove
	glove
	goggles
	javelin
	oar
	pad
	riding jacket
	rifle
	rings
	shorts
	shuttlecock
	skate
	ski
	stick
	sword (foil)
	weights

A2 Guess the sport.

1 Work in groups of four.

2 Take turns to choose one of the sports in A1, but do not say which.

3 Describe a person playing the sport and the equipment he/she is using.

4 The others guess which sport it is.

Example:

A He's wearing brightly-coloured trousers.

B Go on! Give us more help.

A He's holding a long piece of metal.

C It's skiing!

A No, it isn't. There's no snow on the ground. There's grass. And there's a small white ball on the grass.

D It's golf!

A3 Famous sportsmen and women

1 Describe the man and woman in the pictures.
2 Think of another famous sports personality.
Describe him/her to the class.

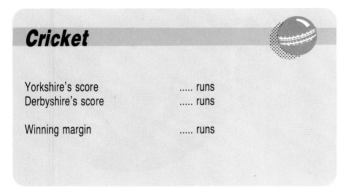

A4 Who is the greatest?

Write down who you think is the best sportsman
and sportswoman for each sport. Discuss your
opinions with the rest of the class.

Sport	Sportsman	Sportswoman
Football		
Skiing		
Cycling		
Athletics		
Swimming		
Skating		
Gymnastics		
Tennis		

A5 📼 Sports report

Listen to the sports report and write down the
results.

Football

Canon League Division 1

Liverpool	. . . | . . .	Southampton
Nottingham Forest	. . . | . . .	Arsenal
Sheffield Wednesday	. . . | . . .	Manchester United

Milk Cup, 1st round

Bradford	. . . | . . .	Middlesbrough
Derby	. . . | . . .	Hartlepool
Hereford	. . . | . . .	Oxford United

Horse racing Goodwood, 5.0

Horses	Place	Starting Prices
Sailor's Song	....	....
Dolly	....	....
Black Prince	....	....
Sam Speed	....	....
Electro	....	....
Lucky Girl	....	....

Cricket

Yorkshire's score	..... runs
Derbyshire's score	..... runs
Winning margin	..... runs

Athletics Helsinki, 1500 metres

Runners	Place
P. Levisse (Fr.)	....
H. Bergen (FRG)	....
S. Ovett (GB)	....
D. Caponi (It.)	....
S. Coe (GB)	....
T. Pinero (Sp.)	....
Winner's time:	....

A6 Sports discussion

gymnastics	chess	cricket	cycling
boxing	football	wind surfing	fox hunting
wrestling	shooting	bull fighting	darts
horse racing	climbing	skiing	car racing
sailing	sky diving	horse riding	swimming

1 Have you ever taken part in any of these sports?

2 How many of these sports do you like?

3 Discuss which of these sports you do . . .
   a inside or outside
   b on water or in the air
   c with an animal
   d with a ball
   e by yourself/with another person/in a team

4 Which sport do you think is . . .
   a the most difficult?
   b the most dangerous?
   c the easiest?
   d the most exciting?
   e the most boring?
    f the cheapest?
   g the most expensive?

5 Compare the different sports like this:

Chess is not *as* exciting *as* sky diving.

I think that boxing is *more* dangerous *than* wrestling.

B Work and leisure

doing   Unit 9, A–B

B1 What does he do? What's he doing now?
Read and study.

What does John McEnroe do?
He plays tennis.
What's he doing now?
He's playing a guitar.

B2 Talk or write about the pictures. Say what the people do and what they are doing now.

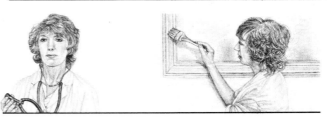

B3 Jack Longland, a furniture restorer, is re-polishing an old table. He describes how he does it to a radio reporter. Listen to the interview and number the pictures 1-6 in the right order. Then try to write a caption for each picture; the first one has been done for you.

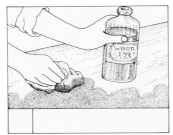

1 Stripping the table

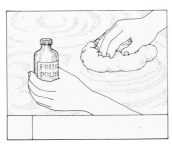
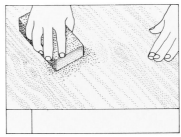
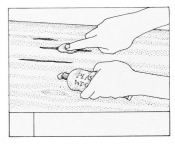

C Time for a break

Your class are the organizers of a scheme called 'Holidays for the Elderly'. You want to arrange a holiday for a group of elderly people coming from Liverpool to your town for a week.

Make five committees. Each committee should complete one of the tasks below.

When the committees have finished their tasks, you should all meet together for an organizers' meeting.

A member of each committee should present a short report of their discussions so that the Chairperson (your teacher) can check that the old people are going to have the best possible time.

Committee 1

Write a letter of invitation to the old people to find out how many of them are interested in the holiday.

Committee 2

Write a letter of information for the people who are coming. Say what the travel arrangements are (coach and train times) and where they are going to stay.

Committee 3

Make a diary of events for the visitors, e.g. entertainments, coach tours, local places to visit. N.B. There is a 'welcome party' on the first evening.

Committee 4

Write a description of the guide who is going to meet them when they arrive and look after them during their stay. Say why you think he/she is an excellent person to do this job.

Committee 5

Arrange a 'welcome party' for the first evening. Make a note of the food, drink and entertainment you want.

11 ▶ ▶ THINKING BACK ▶ ▶ 11

Talking about the past   Holidays   Fables   Nursery rhymes

A Where were you? What was it like?

A1 📼 Monday morning on the bus. Listen and study.

> I went hang-gliding yesterday.
>
> Did you? What was it like?
>
> Oh, it was fantastic!
>
> Weren't you frightened?
>
> Well, I was at first.

A2 Where were you when I phoned?

Work in groups. Take turns to think of a place where you were yesterday when your friend phoned. The other people in your group must guess where you were by asking questions like these:

Were you

> on the beach?
> on a coach tour?
> on a train?

> at home?
> at the hairdresser's?
> at the cinema?
> at a disco?
> at work?

> in a restaurant?
> in the pub?
> in the library?
> in class?

Only answer 'yes' or 'no'!

B What did you do?

B1 📼 Friday afternoon at work. Listen and study. What did Bob do last weekend? What did Liz do?

> What did you do last weekend?
>
> I visited a .... and went to a ....
>
> Did you enjoy it?   No, I didn't.
>
> What about you, Liz?
>
> I watched .... and played ....
>
> Did you win?   Yes, I did.

B2 Ask each other these questions:

What did you do	last night?
	last Saturday?
	last Friday night?
	the day before yesterday?
	last week?
	two days ago?

Some verbs

arrived played stayed visited walked
watched worked

ate bought did drank had saw went

C Could you answer some questions?

C1 🔈 Listen to the dialogue and write down the man's answers to the policeman's questions.

MIDLANDS CONSTABULARY

Where did you go on Saturday?

....

Why did you go there?

....

How did you get there?

....

Who did you go with?

....

What else did you do there?

....

When did you leave?

....

C2 Find out what the other people in the class did last weekend/yesterday/last Friday etc.

C3 Who did something interesting? Tell the rest of the class some of the things people did and the places they went to.

D Did you have a good time?

D1 🔈 Outside the travel agency. Listen and study.

Have you ever been to India?

Yes, I have actually.

How long ago was that?

It was about three years ago.

You lucky thing! How long were you there for?

About two months altogether.

Lovely! Where did you stay?

In small hotels mostly.

Did you see a lot?

Oh yes. I went all over the place.

How did you travel about the country?

By train and bus.

Did you have a good time?

Marvellous. I'm going again when I've got enough money!

D2 Put the words into the right boxes.

by train	in a villa	in a farmhouse
by bike	in a guesthouse	on ferries
in a bed and breakfast	by car	on foot
with a family	in hotels	hitch-hiked

Where did you stay?	How did you travel about?

D3 Ask about the countries your partner has been to.

E Last year's holiday

E1 Holiday survey

First write the questions in column A. Then put your partner's answers in column B.

	A	B
1 Place/Country:	Where did you go?	
2 Length of stay:		
3 Date:		
4 Travel Arrangements: 1 to get there		
2 on holiday		
5 Accommodation:		
6 Activities: 1 sports		
2 places of interest		
7 Cost:		
8 Your opinion:		

E2 You are all at a party. Talk to the other people in your group about your holiday. Ask them about their holidays. Who do you think had the best holiday?

The FOX and the CROW

F Stories of the past

F1 This picture tells the story of a famous fable. Discuss the story. Write sentences for each of the five parts of the picture.

F2 Do you know any other fables? Tell your group.

F3 These nursery rhymes and riddles are poems told to small children in Britain. Some of them are very old. Some of them are songs. Which rhyme or riddle belongs to which picture?

Two bodies have I,
Though both joined in
  one.
The stiller I stand,
The faster I run.

Hot cross buns! Hot cross buns!
One a penny, two a penny,
Hot cross buns!
If your daughters do not
  like them
Give them to your sons;
And if you have not any
  of these pretty little elves,
You cannot do better than
  eat them yourselves.

Doctor Foster went to
  Gloucester
In a shower of rain.
He stepped in a puddle,
Right up to his middle,
And never went there again.

Jack and Jill
Went up the hill,
To fetch a pail of water;
Jack fell down,
And broke his crown,
And Jill came tumbling
  after.

A What's it like?

A1 🔲 At the Lost Property Office. Listen and study.

A2 These are the umbrellas in the Lost Property Office. Which one belongs to the woman in *A1*?

Now find the umbrellas which match these descriptions:

It's a small, red umbrella with black spots on it.

It's a small, plain blue umbrella with a round handle.

It's a big, green umbrella with yellow flowers on it.

It's a big, white umbrella with black stripes and a straight handle.

A3 Read and study.

It's a	long, short, square, triangular, round, pointed, oval, cylindrical,	red blue orange yellow green brown	scarf hat	with	white grey pink	stripes spots bands flowers pictures	on it.	It's made of	silk. cotton. wool. nylon. leather. felt. straw.

A4 Work in pairs. Look at the pictures.

A You have lost your scarf and your hat. Describe them to the person in the Lost Property Office.

B You are the person in the Lost Property Office. Ask for a description of the hat and the scarf, and find them.

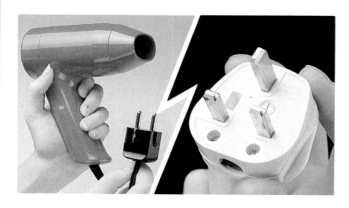

B What's it for?

B1 🔲 It's difficult when you stay with other people. Perhaps your room hasn't got everything you need. Can you say what you need? Listen and study.

Fill the two spaces.

> Can I have a thing for opening a bottle of wine?

> You mean a .... ? Yes, of course.

> Thanks. And I also need a thing for my hair-drier.

> What do you mean? What sort of 'thing'?

> It's a thing made of plastic and metal.

> What's it for?

> It's for connecting things to electricity.

> Oh, you mean a .... !

B2 Match the name of the object with its picture. Then match the picture with its use. They are all things you might need in your room.

It's called . . .

1	a waste-paper basket
☐	a light bulb
☐	an iron
☐	a kettle
☐	a hot-water bottle
☐	a dustpan and brush
☐	a hanger
☐	a tin-opener

It's used for . . .

☐	lighting a room
☐	pressing clothes
☐	hanging clothes on
☐	sweeping the floor
☐	boiling water
1	throwing rubbish away
☐	warming a bed
☐	opening tins

B3 What is it?

1 Choose one of the objects in the pictures.
2 Write a description of it, as in the examples. (The names of the objects are at the bottom of the page.)

It's about 20 centimetres long. It's made of metal, and it's got a wooden handle. It's used for opening bottles of wine.

It's a ....

It's about 5 centimetres long and 1 centimetre wide. It's made of metal. One end is often round and the other end is long and thin. It's used for opening doors.

It's a ....

Now work with a partner.

3 Find out what your partner's object is by asking questions.
4 Choose another object and start again.

How long is it?	What colour is it?
How wide is it?	What's it made of?
How thick is it?	What's it used for?

Examples: corkscrew, key; **1** pencil sharpener; **2** needle; **3** dustbin; **4** safety pin; **5** ashtray; **6** screwdriver; **7** lamp; **8** blanket; **9** scissors

>> 13 >>> >> SORRY! >>> >> 13

Apologizing   Offering to do something   Complaining   Accidents in the home

A I'm sorry!

A1 🔲 In the street. Listen and study.

Why wasn't Jane outside the cinema yesterday?
Why didn't she phone Frank?

> What happened to you yesterday? We arranged to meet outside the cinema.

> Yes, I'm sorry I wasn't there. My .... came ....

> That's O.K.

> And I'm sorry I didn't phone you. I didn't ....

> Never mind.

A2 In pairs, apologize to your partner and give a reason.

I'm sorry I . . .	but I . . .	
didn't do my homework	forgot. didn't have time. lost my book.	Don't worry! It doesn't matter. Never mind! That's all right.
didn't come to your party	had a headache. went away for the weekend. lost the address.	
was late for school	overslept. missed the bus. went to the dentist's.	
didn't meet you last night	had some letters to write. was too tired. lost my way.	

B I've just broken a glass

B1 📼 Listen and study.

B2 You've just done these things!

spilt the tea	scratched the table
burnt the carpet	dirtied the tablecloth
trodden on the cat	knocked over a vase
torn the curtains	smashed a window

Work in pairs. Apologize to your landlady.

A I'm │ very / terribly / awfully │ sorry, │ Maggy, Mrs Clarke, │ but I've just spilt the tea.

B Oh dear!

A I *am* sorry!

B Oh well, │ never mind! / that's all right. / it could happen to anyone. / not to worry.

or

Oh, │ that's a pity! / how did *that* happen?

C Offering to put things right

C1 📼 Listen and study.

I'm awfully sorry, but I've just broken a glass.

Oh well, not to worry.

I'll buy another one this afternoon.

No, that's all right.

Please! Let me buy another one.

Well, all right, thank you.

C2 Match the problems with the solutions.

sellotape	☐
mend it	
jeweller's shop	☐
get it mended	
record shop	☐
pay for a new one	
bar	1
buy another one	
dry cleaner's	☐
get it cleaned	
cloth	☐
clean it up	

C3 Apologize to your partner for doing the things in *C2*. Offer to put them right.

'I'm awfully sorry, Bruce, but I've just spilt your beer. I'll go to the bar and buy another one.'

C4 Work in pairs. Take turns to be A and B.
Make conversations for the five situations.

	A	B
1	You're at a disco and you've just spilt beer down the person at the next table. You trod on his/her foot as well on the dance floor!	You are at a disco. The girl/man at the next table has just spilt beer all over you! He/she trod on your foot as well while dancing.
2	You went to London for the weekend. You promised to write to your friend but you didn't have time. You don't want to quarrel with your friend.	Your friend went to London last week and promised to write you a letter, but he/she didn't. You were disappointed.
3	You were late for classes all last week, because you work in a hotel at night, and you were too tired. You don't want to tell your teacher the real reason in case they send you off the course.	You are a teacher. A student in your class was late every morning last week. You want to know why.
4	You are living with a family. You had a few friends in your room last night. They stayed late and made a lot of noise.	You are a landlady/landlord. Your student had some friends in his/her room last night. They made a lot of noise and woke the baby. It's the first time this has happened. You like your student.
5	You are a waiter in a restaurant. Several of the kitchen staff are away from work, ill. The meals are taking a long time to prepare.	You are a customer in a restaurant. Tonight the service is very slow. You are disappointed as it's your wife/husband's birthday.

D Complaining

D1 😐 English people say 'sorry' a lot, both for apologizing and before saying something unpleasant, e.g. to make a complaint. Listen and study.

D2 Work in groups. Take turns to be the manager and the guests. The guests make the complaint ('I'm sorry but . . .') and the manager offers a solution. Here are the complaints:

Your room is too hot.	There's no one behind the bar, and you want a drink.
The porter was rude to you.	Your room is too cold.
There aren't any sheets on the bed.	The service is too slow in the restaurant.
The lift isn't working.	There's only one bed in your room and you wanted two.
There's a horrible smell in your bathroom.	The waiter brought you coffee and you wanted tea.
The people in the next room are making too much noise.	The food is *awful*!

A *The British food year*

What do British people eat at Christmas? Is it the same in your country?

What festivals are most important in your country?

Do you eat anything special at festivals and holidays in your country?

THE — B·R·I·T·I·S·H FOOD YEAR

We often eat special food at festivals and holidays.

January 1st
In Scotland people often eat shortbread.

January 25th
Burns Night, again in Scotland. Haggis is always cooked for dinner on this night.

Shrove Tuesday
Pancake Day

Ash Wednesday
The first day of Lent, a period when many people try not to eat so much of their favourite food!

Good Friday
Hot cross buns.

Easter Sunday
Chocolate Easter eggs are often given as presents. Boiled eggs are often eaten. New season spring lamb is often on the menu. Simnel Cake is a special Easter cake.

October 31st
Halloween. Hot soup and baked potatoes, toffee apples.

November 5th
Bonfire Night. Parkin, a spicy cake, is often served. Potatoes, sausages and chestnuts are cooked in the bonfire.

December 25th
Christmas Day. Roast turkey, chestnut stuffing, roast potatoes, Brussels sprouts, bread sauce and gravy – followed by Christmas pudding, followed by Christmas cake, followed by a long sleep!

December 31st
New Year's Eve. In Scotland this is a big occasion and they usually eat haggis, turnips and potatoes ('neeps' and 'tatties') and drink lots of whisky.

B Sherry trifle

B1 🔊 Sherry trifle has been a very popular pudding in Britain for hundreds of years. It is often eaten on special occasions.·

Listen to the recording and write down the quantities of the ingredients.

B2 🔊 Below are some pictures to show you how to make sherry trifle. The pictures are in the right order but the instructions are jumbled. Listen to the recording, work with a partner and match the pictures with the method.

Ingredients for Sherry Trifle

Sponge cake	.....	
Raspberry jam	..... g	
Sherry	..... ml	
Raspberries	..... g	
	or	

Custard:
milk	..... ml
vanilla essence	..... tsp
eggs	.....
egg yolks	.....
sugar	.....

Double cream	..... ml
Split almonds	..... g
Glacé cherries	..... g

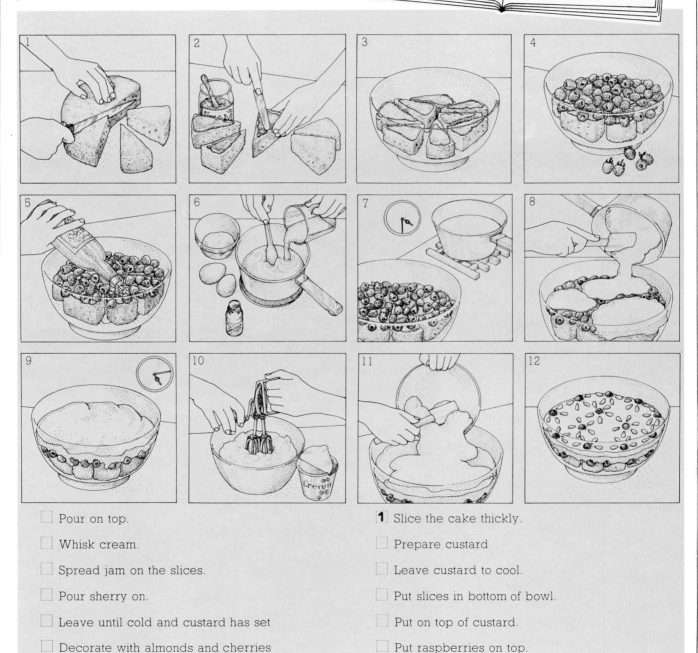

☐ Pour on top.	**1** Slice the cake thickly.
☐ Whisk cream.	☐ Prepare custard
☐ Spread jam on the slices.	☐ Leave custard to cool.
☐ Pour sherry on.	☐ Put slices in bottom of bowl.
☐ Leave until cold and custard has set	☐ Put on top of custard.
☐ Decorate with almonds and cherries	☐ Put raspberries on top.

B3 Custard, known in many countries as 'English cream', is quite difficult to make. Read and study this chart.

Link words	Method	Ingredients
First	beat	the eggs with sugar and milk.
Next	heat	the rest of the milk until lukewarm.
Then	beat	the milk into the eggs.
After that	cook	slowly until the mixture thickens. Do not boil.
Then	stir	in the vanilla essence.
Finally	serve	hot or cold.

Pat Cooper is showing a Swedish visitor, Gunilla, how to make custard.

🔊 Listen to the recording and fill in the missing parts of the conversation, using the chart above.

Pat Right then, Gunilla – first you ....
Gunilla OK. First I ....
Pat Then you must ....
Gunilla Mmm. What do I have to do now?
Pat Next you have to ....
Gunilla I see, and what then?
Pat Ah, now comes the difficult bit. You should .... until it .... but you must *not* ....
Gunilla Right, I'll be careful. That seems all right. What's next?
Pat Nearly finished now. All you have to do is ....
Gunilla Good. There we are! Mmm, I think English custard is lovely!

B4 Give instructions on how to make your favourite dishes, using the link words in *B3*.

C Keeping fit

If you eat a lot, you may put on weight. You could go on a diet or do some exercises to keep your body healthy.

C1 🔊 Diet. Pat Cooper has a weight problem. She gets advice from her doctor. Listen and study. Supply the verbs in the blanks.

> Don't .... too many potatoes, but .... lots of fresh vegetables.

> I see. Lots of vegetables, no potatoes.

> Always .... vegetable oil for frying foods. Never .... with animal fats.

> OK, no fats. What about meat?

> Well, a reasonable amount. And .... careful with dairy products.

C2 Work in pairs. Read the following lists and make up more conversations like the one in *C1*.

Quantities	Fattening foods	'Reasonable' foods	Non-fattening foods
too many . . .	potatoes	eggs	green vegetables
too much . . .	bread	butter	fresh fruit
lots of . . .	pasta	cheese	vegetable oil
a lot of . . .	animal fats	milk	fish
a reasonable amount of . . .	sugar	lean meat	unsweetened yoghurt
only a little . . .	sweet puddings		
only a few . . .	cream		
no . . .			

C3 Exercise. Match the pictures with the instructions.

☐ For spine and balance. Raise alternate knees to meet forehead. Keep supporting leg slightly bent. (Normally weight should never be on heels.)

☐ For trunk muscles and lower back. Sit, legs apart and parallel, feet relaxed, rib cage well lifted. Bend sideways without 'rotating'. Hold.

☐ For upper thighs and buttocks. Both knees facing forward. Lift upper leg till pelvis begins to lift sideways. Twist upper leg.

☐ For back muscles, buttocks, backs of thighs and arms. Feet pointed, hands clasped. Lift chest, arms and legs at the same time. Look up and hold.

☐ For abdomen and lower back. Knees bent, feet apart. Begin with small of back well into floor, pelvis tilted upwards. Raise hips, then upper back.

C4 Health farm

Work in groups of four. You all work at a Health Farm. At your daily meeting you discuss your problem clients.

Two of you are keep-fit instructors. Choose exercises for each client.

Two of you are dieticians. Plan a suitable diet for each client.

1 A middle-aged businessman with an ulcer.
2 An active pensioner.
3 A man who is convalescing after an accident.
4 An overweight housewife.
5 A film star who needs a rest.

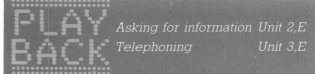

A Hotel accommodation

PLAY BACK

Asking for information Unit 2,E
Telephoning   Unit 3,E

A1 These signs are taken from a hotel guide. Find out what they mean.

A2 Find out the following information about a four-star hotel, a two-star hotel and a 'bed and breakfast' in your area.

	★★★★ Hotel	★★ Hotel	B & B
1 How much does a single room cost?			
And a double room?			
2 Have the rooms got private bathrooms?			
3 Is the hotel licensed?			
4 Does it offer full board?			
Half board?			
Bed and breakfast only?			
5 Is there a car park?			
6 Are there any other facilities (swimming pool, tennis court, TV lounge etc.)?			

A3 Work in pairs.

A	B
Imagine you want to stay somewhere in your area. You are not quite sure what kind of accommodation you want. Ring the Accommodation Agency to ask if they can help you.	Imagine you work in an Accommodation Agency. Using the information in A2, try to help the caller.

B Booking into a hotel

B1 🔊 Listen and study.

Put ticks in the chart for the Smiths' accommodation.

	with bath	without bath
Single room		
Double room, double bed		
Double room, twin beds		

Receptionist Good evening, sir. Can I help you?
Mr Smith Yes. I'd like rooms for three people, my daughter, my wife and myself, please.
Receptionist Certainly, sir. Singles, or a double and a single?
Mr Smith Could I have one single and one double room, please?
Receptionist Certainly. The double room has twin beds.
Mr Smith That's fine. Are they with or without bathrooms?

Receptionist Both rooms have bathrooms, en suite.
Mr Smith Good. I'll take them.
Receptionist Very good, sir. That's one single room with bath and one double room with bath. Could you sign the register, please, sir? Thank you. Here are your keys. I'll call the porter for you.
Mr Smith Thank you very much. Oh, may I use your telephone for a moment?
Receptionist Certainly, sir. It's over there.

B2 The hotel is full until tomorrow! Repeat the conversation, but change it to make sense in these situations:

1 The receptionist apologizes and offers rooms for the next day. The Smiths accept the offer.

2 The Smiths say they are sorry, but they need somewhere for tonight. The receptionist gives them the name of another hotel. They decide to try it.

B3 The Smiths go to the hotel restaurant for dinner. It isn't a very good restaurant.

1 Make two groups.
2 Read the card for your group.
3 Discuss what to say with the rest of your group.
4 Find a partner from the other group. Act out the conversation.

Group A

You are Mr Smith or Mrs Smith. Complain to the waiter/waitress about the things wrong with the restaurant:

– the soup's cold
– the meat's tough
– the service is slow
– the place is dark
– the knives are dirty etc.

Group B

You are the waiter or waitress. Apologize to the Smiths and offer to put things right. There are some problems tonight:

– the cook is sick
– the manager's wife is doing the cooking and she doesn't like cooking very much
– there is a power cut etc.

C Holiday camps

Asking about experiences	Unit 7,A
Asking about the past	Unit 11,D
Instructions	Unit 14
Prepositions	Unit 2,B

C1 Holiday camps are very popular in Britain. They provide facilities for almost everything you might want to do during a holiday.

Match the pictures with the activities.

French bowls
swimming pool
pony-trekking
wind-surfing
sight-seeing tours
fishing
volleyball
Mini-Clubs for the kids
walking and climbing
discos
keep-fit
tennis courts
sailing
playgrounds
mini-golf
rest and relaxation

C2 Find someone who . . .

Ask the other students if they have ever done any of the activities in *C1*. If they say yes, ask them when they did it and if they enjoyed it.

Have you ever	been to a holiday camp?
	tried wind-surfing?
	played French bowls?
	ridden a horse?

C3 You are an instructor in the holiday camp's mini-club. You are teaching the kids how to make a model glider. Study the diagrams and the other information, and then tell the rest of the class (the 'kids'!) what to do.

Useful vocabulary

Link words	Verbs	
First	make	glue
Then	cut	join
Next	use	paint
After that	fit	
Finally	shape	

Materials needed

Balsa wood (15mm, 5mm and 3mm thick)
Piece of rubber or elastic
Paint

Equipment needed

Sharp knife or razor blade
Sandpaper
Glue

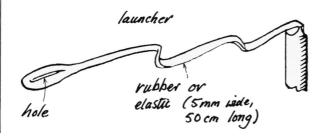

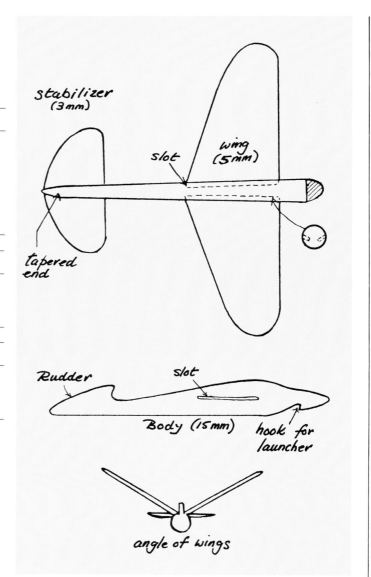

C4 Prepositions

Fill each blank with one of the prepositions.

Jack went .... the house and launched his glider .... the air. It flew .... to a height of 5 metres, ... some trees and .... the garden fence. Then it glided .... the field, ... some cows, and came .... on the grass .... the river.

through	across	up	out of	down
near	into		past	over

D Alien!

PLAY BACK

Telling a story   Unit 11,F
Describing things   Unit 12

D1 In groups, write sentences to tell the story in the pictures.

Compare your story with other groups.

Write the best story on the blackboard, or for your homework.

D2 Work in groups. Take turns to be the creature from Outer Space. While you were on Earth, you went into a department store. You saw many things but you can't remember the names. Describe one thing that you saw. The rest of the group tries to guess what it is you are describing by asking questions.

A Motoring laws

A1 The law says:

YOU MUSTN'T DRIVE WITHOUT A SEATBELT

Make statements about other things you mustn't do in a car in Britain, e.g.

drive/lights/night

You mustn't drive without lights at night.

1 drive/right-hand side/road
2 park/double yellow lines
3 drive/more/70 m.p.h.
4 do/U-turn/motorway

5 ....

6 ....

fasten your seatbelt NOW PLEASE

A2 Where can you see this notice?

PASSENGERS MUST NOT

1. **Stand forward of this notice.**

2. **Speak to the driver without due cause or distract his attention while vehicle is in motion.**

3. **Leave luggage in any gangway.**

Which book is this from?

You must not	
— stop your cycle within the limits of a pedestrian crossing, except in circumstances beyond your control or when it is necessary to do so to avoid an accident;	**PPCRGD** No 12 and **ZPCR** No 9
— on the approach to an uncontrolled Zebra crossing marked by a pattern of zigzag lines, overtake the moving motor vehicle nearest to the crossing or the leading vehicle which has stopped to give way to a pedestrian on the crossing;	**ZPCR** No 10
— ride recklessly;	**RTA 1972** Sect 17
— ride without due care and attention or without reasonable consideration for other persons using the road;	**RTA 1972** Sect 18
— ride under the influence of drink or a drug;	**RTA 1972** Sect 19
— wilfully ride on a footpath by the side of any road made or set apart for the use of foot passengers;	**HA 1835** Sect 72 **RB(S)A** Sch C and **BP(S)A** Sect 381 (40)
— by negligence or misbehaviour interrupt the free passage of any road user or vehicle;	**HA 1835** Sect 78 **BP(S)A** Sect 381 (10)
— leave your cycle on any road in such a way that it is likely to cause danger to other road users;	**RTA 1972** Sect 24
— leave your cycle where waiting is prohibited;	**RTRA** Sects 1, 6 and 9

B Legal documents

B1  At the police station. Listen and study.
Supply the three missing words.

> What documents must you have if you own a car?
>
> You must have a .... licence.
>
> Yes, of course. What else do you have to have?
>
> You have to have an .... certificate and .... tax.

B2 What documents do you have to have in Britain
if you want to . . .

1 own a TV?
2 travel abroad?
3 show how old you are?
4 travel cheaply as a student?
5 own a dog?
6 pay a restaurant bill by cheque?
7 show that you are married?
8 work?

B3 What do you have to do if you have a car
accident?

C Telling yourself to do something

C1  In the school corridor. Listen and study.

C2 What do you tell yourself in these situations?

1 You haven't got any money.

2 Your telephone bill has arrived.

3 Your passport has expired.

4 Your tooth is aching.

5 The house is a mess and your mother's coming
to tea.

D It's optional

D1 🔊 In the school café. Listen and study.

> Do you have to go to all the lessons?
>
> No, you needn't if you don't want to.
>
> What about extra lab?
>
> You don't have to do that. It's optional.

D2 In Britain there are things you don't have to do.

You	don't have to / needn't	vote.

Make statements about other things you don't have to do in Britain.
1 carry an identity card
2 go to school after 16
3 have babies in hospital
4 do military service
5 get married in church
6 ....
7 ....
8 ....

D3 And in your country? Discuss like this:

> Do you have to vote in your country?
>
> Yes, we do.   *or*   No, we don't.

E Mustn't? Needn't?

Make sentences for each picture, as in the examples.

IN THE INTEREST OF HYGIENE
NO SMOKING IN THIS STORE

You mustn't smoke.

Evening Meal Optional

You needn't have an evening meal.

NO PARKING

1 park

KEEP OFF THE GRASS

2 walk

Black Tie Optional

3 wear

NO BATHING

4 swim

5 drive

FREE CAR PARK

6 pay

NO EXIT

7 go out

HOTEL BAR Open to non-residents

8 be a resident

WILL PATRONS KINDLY REFRAIN FROM:

RUNNING   PUSHING   ACROBATICS OR GYMNASTICS

SHOUTING   DUCKING   PETTING

BOMBING   SWIMMING IN DIVING AREA   SMOKING

F It's not allowed!

F1 🔲 At the swimming pool. Listen and study.

What two things are you not allowed to do?

You're not allowed to .... in here.
Oh, sorry!
You can't .... in here. It's too dangerous.
Oh, that's a stupid rule.

F2 What else can't you do in the swimming pool?

F3 In groups, make a list of rules for your class. Report back to the rest of the class. Do you have the same rules as other groups? Are rules necessary?

F4 You are the parent of a seven-year-old called Peter. Peter is going to stay with his grandmother for a few days. There are some rules for Peter that you want her to know.

Complete the statements.

1 eat/sweets/between meals
2 watch/horror films/TV
3 ride/bicycle/road
4 play with matches
5 stay up/late

>> 17 >> HOW DO YOU FEEL? >> 17

Expressing feelings   Congratulating   Sympathizing   Emotions   Good news and bad news   Optimism and pessimis

A Describing feelings

A1 Read and study.

He She	is looks feels	sad sorry bored puzzled worried	frightened angry proud excited happy

A2 Describe how each person feels, using the words in *A1*.

| Joe Biggs | Susie | Mr James | Jackie | Pete |

| Rod | Bob | Tom | Pat | Janet |

What is the situation in each picture?
What is each person saying or thinking?

A3 Discuss how you feel in these situations.

How do you feel when

- you have to take an examination?
- you walk through a forest at night?
- you see a horror film?
- you do homework?

- you pass a test?
- you get up in the morning?
- you go on holiday?

....

....

B It's the way that you say it

B1 🔲 The way you say something is important for expressing feelings. Listen to the dialogues between Pete and Susie. You'll hear the same words twice. Decide how Susie feels from the way she answers Pete. Put a cross in the chart.

A Pete What's the matter?
Susie Nothing.

B Pete Are you all right?
Susie Yes, of course.

B2 Work in pairs. Practise the dialogues together. Try to decide which emotion your partner is expressing by the way he/she answers the questions.

Dialogue	A		B	
Susie is . . .	1	2	1	2
happy				
surprised at the question				
angry				
sad				
excited				
frightened				

C Asking about feelings

C1 🔲 Listen to these conversations. Fill the spaces.

A

Sam You look ....
George Yes, I am.
Sam Why's that?
George Well, I'm on holiday.
Sam Really? .... you!
George Yes, and I'm going off on my own for a few days.
Sam How nice for you!

B

Sally You look a bit ....
Linda Yes, I am.
Sally Why? What's wrong?
Linda Well, the trouble is, George never listens to me.
Sally Oh dear! ....you!
Linda And not only that but he's going on holiday without me.
Sally How miserable for you!

C2 Work in pairs. Take turns to be A or B and make conversations like these for the situations below.

A You look . . .	**A** You look a bit . . .
B Yes, I am.	**B** Yes, I am.
A Why's that?	**A** Why? What's wrong?
B Well, . . .	**B** Well, the trouble is . . .
A Really? Lucky you!	**A** Oh dear! Poor you!

	A	B
Situation 1	You meet your friend in the pub. You think he looks rather miserable so you ask him why.	Your friend comes into the pub. You don't feel like talking because you've just lost your job.
Situation 2	Your friend is unemployed. He/she usually looks unhappy but today he/she is singing! Ask why.	You've got a job at last. It's well-paid and very interesting. You're going to be an astronaut. Tell your friend.
Situation 3	Your friend looks very excited about something. Find out what it is.	You've just won a competition. You're going to travel around the Far East for six weeks. You're really excited. You see a friend.

D Making the right noises

D1 🔊 Listen and study.

D2 🔊 Look at the conversations in *C1* again. Notice how Sam and Sally express interest and sympathy in what George and Linda tell them. Listen again to the phrases they use:

Good news	Bad news
Really? Lucky you!	Oh dear! Poor you!
How nice for you!	How miserable for you!

D3 Which of the following are answers to good news and which to bad news? Put a tick (✓) for good news and a cross (✗) for bad news. (Two of them could be good or bad.)

Thank goodness! ○
That's terrible! ○
Don't worry! ○
Great! ○
What a shame! ○
Incredible! ○
Try not to worry! ○
I am sorry! ○
Never mind! ○
It'll be all right! ○
Well done! ○
That's marvellous! ○
Oh dear! ○
How awful! ○
Oh no! ○
What a pity! ○
Congratulations! ○
Really? ○

D4 Work in pairs. You are A or B. Cover up your partner's card. Your partner will tell you some news. Reply with one of the phrases in *D3*.

A Tell your partner that . . .
1 Your dog has just died.
2 You've passed your driving test.
3 You're worried about the exam tomorrow.
4 You've lost your passport and all your money.
5 You've won a free trip to Los Angeles.

B Tell your partner that . . .
1 You saw a UFO last night.
2 You've crashed your car.
3 You've just got engaged.
4 You've just got a new job.
5 You've scratched your partner's favourite record.

E Optimists and pessimists

E1 😀 I'm really looking forward to it!

Listen and study. Who is the optimist and who is the pessimist?

I'm really looking forward to going to London.

Are you? I'm not. I can't stand visiting noisy cities.

But London is so fantastic, so exciting. I'm really fascinated by the historical monuments. It'll be wonderful.

I hate visiting old buildings. I'm really NOT looking forward to going at all. It'll be terrible.

E2 Work in pairs. You are going on a camping holiday. One of you loves camping, the other hates it. Discuss the holiday using these ideas and phrases to help you:

cooking over an open fire
walking
sleeping in a tent
birds and animals

wild flowers
peaceful/too quiet
healthy/cold and wet
relaxing/uncomfortable

I'm looking forward to ....ing
I'm interested in ....ing
I'm fascinated by ....
It's great/marvellous
It's so ....
It'll be wonderful

I hate ....ing
I can't stand ....ing
I'm bored by ....ing
It's awful/miserable
It's too ....
It'll be terrible

E3 🔲 Don't worry!

Listen and study. Who is Mrs Brown worried about?

E4 Work in pairs. You are A or B. Take turns to discuss your problem, using these phrases:

I hope . . .
(He) might be . . .
Where on earth can (he) be?
What on earth has happened to (him)?
Do you think I should . . . ?

Don't worry.
Try not to worry.
I'm sure . . .
(He's) probably . . .
It'll be all right.

A

Your son is 16. He has gone on a climbing holiday with a friend. He left two weeks ago and he hasn't written to you yet.

B

Your daughter is 17. She is acting very strangely these days. She stays out late every night, looks miserable and never talks to you. She is usually so happy. Now she is missing from home. You last saw her two days ago.

F *What's your favourite?*

Tell the people in your group about
1 your favourite painting
2 your favourite piece of music
3 your favourite poem or story

How do you feel when you see, hear or read it?

The Weather

A DEPRESSION with associated frontal troughs will move E across S Britain.

London, SE England, Cent S England, Channel Islands, SW England: Cloudy, occasional rain preceded by snow in places. Wind SW moderate locally fresh, becoming variable light. Rather cold, max 7 or 8C (45 or 46F).

East Anglia, Midlands: Cloudy, outbreaks of sleet or snow, mostly turning to rain. Wind SW, moderate becoming variable light. Cold, max 6 or 7C (43 to 45F).

E England, Wales, NW England, Cent N England: Cloudy, outbreaks of sleet or snow, heavy on hills dying out later. Wind E, backing NE, moderate, locally fresh for a time. Cold, max 6 to 7C (43 to 45F).

Lake District, NE England, Borders, SW Scotland: Rather cloudy, a little snow in places, becoming mainly dry with sunny or clear intervals. Wind variable, light or moderate. Rather cold, max 6 to 8C (43 to 46F).

Isle of Man, N Ireland: Outbreaks of sleet or snow at first, sunny or clear intervals, scattered wintry showers. Wind E, backing to moderate, locally fresh. Rather cold, max 7 or 8C (45 or 46F).

Edinburgh and Dundee, Aberdeen, Glasgow, Moray Firth, Argyll: Mainly dry, sunny periods. Wind variable, mainly N, light or moderate, rather cold, max

AROUND THE WORLD
Lunch-time reports

		C	F
Ajaccio	F	16	61
Akrotiri	Th	15	59
Algiers	S	22	72
Amsterdam	C	5	41
Athens	S	18	64
Bahrain	S	25	77
Barbados	S	30	86
Barcelona	F	17	63
Belgrade	S	20	68
Beirut	Th	11	52
Berlin	F	3	37
Bermuda	Dr	20	68
Biarritz	C	11	52
Birmingham	S	7	45
Bordeaux	C	12	54
Boston	C	6	43
Boulogne	C	6	43
Bristol	F	8	46
Brussels	F	7	45
Budapest	R	10	50
Cairo	S	17	63
Cape Town	F	21	70
Cardiff	C	7	45
Casablanca	C	19	66
Cologne	F	7	45
Copenhagen	F	2	36
Corfu	S	17	63
Dublin	F	8	46
Dubrovnik	S	16	61
Edinburgh	F	7	45
Faro	S	17	63
Florence	C	16	61
Frankfurt	F	6	43
Funchal	F	15	59
Geneva	R	6	43
Gibraltar	R	18	64
Glasgow	C	7	45
Helsinki	F	1	34
Hong Kong	C	25	77
Innsbruck	C	9	48
Inverness	S	6	43
Istanbul	S	11	52
Las Palmas	C	19	66
Lisbon	S	17	63
Locarno	S	16	61
London	S	10	50

		C	F
L Angeles	C	13	55
Luxembrg	F	5	41
Madrid	S	22	72
Majorca	F	18	64
Malaga	Dr	18	64
Malta	S	18	64
Manchester	R	4	39
Melbourne	F	19	66
Miami	F	24	75
Montreal	C	10	50
Moscow	C	0	32
Munich	Sn	3	37
Nairobi	S	29	84
Naples	F	14	57
Newcastle	S	7	45
New York	R	7	45
New Delhi	S	22	72
Nice	S	15	59
Oporto	S	17	63
Oslo	Sl	2	36
Paris	R	8	46
Perth	S	25	77
Prague	F	6	43
Reykjavik	S	-4	25
Rhodes	S	19	66
R de Jan	S	34	93
Rome	C	16	61
Salzburg	R	3	37
S Francisco	F	11	52
Seoul	S	18	64
Singapore	Th	25	77
Stockholm	C	2	36
Strasbourg	R	6	43
Sydney	F	30	86
Tangier	C	18	64
Tenerife	S	21	70
Tokyo	S	17	63
Toronto	R	6	43
Valencia	S	18	64
Vancouver	S	11	52
Venice	F	16	61
Vienna	C	10	50
Washington	Dr	13	52
Wellington	S	18	64
Zurich	C	8	46

C, cloudy; Dr, drizzle; F, fair; Fg, fog; R, rain; S, sunny; Sl, sleet; Sn, snow; Th, thunder.

A The weather

A1 Look at the weather information. Answer the questions.

1 Which city is the coldest?
2 What is the weather like in Edinburgh?
3 Where would you like to be?
4 Why?
5 Is it winter or summer in the UK?
6 Which part of the UK is the warmest?
7 What's the weather like in your town or country?
8 You are going to Barbados. What's the weather like there? What'll you wear?

A2 😐 Listen and study.

I'm sure it's going to rain.

It could turn out wet or fine.

Maybe it'll be warm and sunny.

I think it'll be cold and dull.

Perhaps it'll snow.

It might be windy.

A3 Discuss today's weather. Is it going to change? Do you think it'll rain?

A4 Read the weather forecast.

In small groups, make a weather forecast for your area.

Compare your forecast with other groups.

> **An intense depression is moving east from the Atlantic towards the Channel.**
>
> West Scotland and Northern Ireland will be mostly dry, but other parts could be cloudy with rain or sleet at times, with some snow in Eastern and Central Scotland and on high ground in England and Wales. It will be cold in all areas tomorrow, and might also be very windy.

B What'll you do if it rains?

B1 🔈 At work. Listen and study.
Where is Jim going this weekend? Where will he go if it rains?

> What are you doing this weekend?
>
> I'm going to the ....
>
> What'll you do if it rains?
>
> Oh, I'll go to the ....

B2 Make conversations with a partner, using these ideas:

1 cinema/full/restaurant
2 museum/crowded/go for a walk
3 disco/crowded/go to the pub
4 a party/boring/go home

B3 'Wet blanket'

Work in pairs. One of you is planning a party for the weekend; the other is a 'wet blanket' – he/she can always see problems. Take turns to make proposals and to be the 'wet blanket', as in the example. Here are some more ideas:

Plan
make a hot punch
make a fondue
put lights in the garden
show a video
organize a game of roulette

Problem
you can't use the cooker
you can't find the right sort of cheese
it rains
the TV breaks down
they have no money

Example:
A I'm going to invite all the class, and the teacher too . . .
B What are you going to do if she can't come?
A Well, if she can't come, I'll just invite the others. I'm going to take the furniture out of my room . . .
B What'll you do if your landlady says no?
A Well, if she says no, I'll leave it in. I'm going to . . .

C What'll you do when you finish the course?

C1 🔈 In the school café. Listen and study.
Fill the blanks.

> What'll you do when you finish the course?
>
> Oh, I'll probably take an .... examination.
>
> Really? Will you go to .... classes?
>
> No, I won't. I'd like to take a .... course.

C2 What do you think you'll do in the future? Discuss in groups.

Will you
- take an English examination?
- travel to other countries?
- become famous?
- get rich?
- learn another foreign language?
- .... ?

Would you like to do these things?

C3 When/if

Fill the blanks with either when or if. Then ask your partner the questions.

What are you going to do
What'll you do
- .... it rains this afternoon?
- .... you get home tonight?
- .... you don't finish your homework tonight?
- .... you see your best friend again?
- .... your TV set breaks down tonight?
- .... you have to say goodbye to your landlady?

D Good intentions

D1 Sometimes we have very strong ideas of what we want to do.

> I'm going to learn to drive next year.

In Britain on New Year's Eve we make a list of things we intend to do in the new year. These are called New Year's Resolutions. Have you got a tradition like this?

Imagine it is December 31st. Make ten resolutions, e.g.

> I'm not going to get married.

> I'm going to stop smoking.

D2 Now, in groups, tell your friends your resolutions. Listen to everyone's resolutions and then report to the class, like this:

Miguel is going to give up smoking. Saif and Pierre are going to travel.

January 1st

My Resolutions

1
2
3
4
5
6
7
8
9
10

E What do you think will happen?

E1 In small groups discuss:

Who will win | the next World Cup?
| the most medals at the next Olympic Games?
| the next Wimbledon tennis finals?

E2 Questionnaire

Read through the questions. Put a tick (✓) in one of the columns. Try to think of reasons for your answers. Discuss your answers with other students.

		Sure	Perhaps	No
Do you think	you will ever change your job?			
	you will ever live in another country?			
	everyone will be educated through TV one day?			
	everyone will speak English one day?			
	Britain will ever have a President?			
	nuclear arms will ever be abolished?			
	people will ever live under the sea?			

F Weather poems

F1 🔲 Listen to this poem by Charles Hadfield.

1 Where is the poet, do you think?

2 What time of day is it?

After a sleepless night
(heartbeat, heat
the hoot of long foreign trains
across vast distances)

it would not be good morning without
first birdsong
then clean light
breaking through mist

along the top of the hill
each branch and leaf
sharp against the sky

the sun floating up on the haze where
yesterday I looked out to sea

white silence stretching out to nothing

F2 🔲 Arrange the lines of this poem by Christina Rossetti in the right order. Then listen.

Wandering, whistling to and fro,
Bringing rain out of the west,
The Whistling Wind
From the dim north bringing snow?
O wind, why do you never rest,

F3 🔲 This is another poem by Christina Rossetti. Put the last line of each verse in. Then think of a title for the poem. Then listen.

> The wind has such a rainy sound
>   Moaning through the town,
> The sea has such a windy sound, –
>
>
> The apples in the orchard
>   Tumble from their tree. –
> Oh will the ships go down, go down,

| In the windy sea? | Will the ships go down? |

F4 Have you ever tried to write a poem? Try writing one about the wind or the early morning. It doesn't have to rhyme.

19 ▸ FITNESS AND SURVIVAL ▸ 19

Ability   Possibility   Self-sufficiency   Survival   Travel

A Test your limits

A1 An old man wants to go in for a marathon race. He is talking to his doctor so that he can plan his exercise programme and check on his health and fitness. Listen and study. Fill the spaces.

Can you .... your toes, Mr Jervis?

No, I can't. I'm not very good at bending.

Can you do a .... ?

No, I can get down but I can't get up again.

Can you .... up hills?

Yes, that's no problem.

What about your .... ? Can you see the letters on this card?

Yes, I can see them clearly.

Good. Now, can you .... a bicycle?

No, I don't know how to ride a bicycle.

Oh. What about .... ? Can you do them?

Oh yes, I'm very good at doing press-ups. I can do 40.

A2 Read and study.

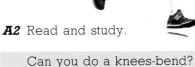

Can you do a knees-bend?		
or	Yes, I can.
	No, I can't.
Are you good at doing press-ups?		
or	Yes, I am.
	No, I'm not.

What about you? Can you do these things? Are you good at doing them?

B Self-sufficiency

B1 Read and study.

Do you know how to make bread?	
or	Yes, I do.
	No, I don't.

Can you skin a rabbit?	
or	Maybe.
	I don't think so.

Some people don't like the modern way of life. They think that city life is unhealthy and that office jobs are boring. They want to return to a simple life in the country where they can grow their own food, make their own clothes and learn to be self-sufficient. Could you be self-sufficient? Complete this questionnaire:

Do you know how to...	Yes, I do	No, I don't
1 milk a cow?		
2 make butter and cheese?		
3 build a house?		
4 decorate a room?		
5 change a plug?		
6 make a table?		
7 make plates and cups?		
8 weave cloth?		
9 make your own clothes?		
10 repair your own shoes?		
11 knit a jumper?		
12 grow your own vegetables?		
13 make bread?		
14 cook good food?		

B2 Interview the people in your class. How many of them know how to do these things?

C Survival course

C1 Read and study.

You can	make a shelter with a plastic sheet.
It's possible to	light a fire with a piece of glass.

Work in groups. You are going on a survival course for a month.

You are going to live on an island where there are no other people. There are no houses and no shops. The island has got trees, a small river, rabbits and other wild food. The weather is very bad. It is often cold and wet.

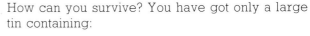

How can you survive? You have got only a large tin containing:

- a plastic sheet
- a knife
- a ball of string
- a box of matches
- a safety pin

Discuss what you can do with these things. How can you . . .

- make a shelter?
- fetch water?
- get food?
- cook food?
- keep warm?

C2 Would you like to go on a survival course? Why/why not?

D Travelling around

There are many different methods of travelling. For example, if you want to get off the island, you can swim! A more comfortable way to get away from the island is by boat, of course.

D1 Look at the pictures and write down the name of the method of travelling. Then work with a partner and discuss the advantages and disadvantages of each method. Which method do you prefer to use? Why? Compare your answers with the other people in the class.

method	advantages	disadvantages

D2 What are you doing after the course? Discuss your travel arrangements with a partner.

D3 Here is part of a letter from one of your friends. Write a reply giving information about your travel arrangements.

Could you let me know when you're arriving and where, so that I can meet you? It'll be marvellous to see you again after all this time. I'm really looking forward to telling you all my news!

Write soon,

E The Ten Tors Expedition

E1 These newspaper articles are about one kind of survival course. Work in pairs. One person reads article A, the other reads article B.

A Before the event

Make notes to answer these questions:
1 How many people are there in each team?
2 What do the competitors wear? Why?
3 How far must they walk?
4 What must they carry?

Use your notes to tell your partner about the expedition. Ask him/her what happened in 1983.

B What happened in 1983?

Make notes to answer these questions:
1 How many people didn't finish?
2 What problems did they have?
3 Who came first in each section?
35 miles? 45 miles? 55 miles?

Use your notes to tell your partner what happened. Ask him/her about the rules of the expedition.

TEN TORS ENTRY LIMITED TO 2,400

MORE THAN 2,000 young walkers are taking part today and tomorrow in the 24th annual Ten Tors Expedition on Dartmoor.

The massed start at Okehampton Camp provides a spectacular sight as the 2,400 walkers, all aged between 14 and 19, and wearing brightly-coloured safety clothing, set off to cover some of the wildest and most beautiful moorland in the Westcountry. More walkers wanted to enter this year but the number has been restricted to 400 teams of six to protect the countryside and for safety.

The Ten Tors is an adventurous event demanding endurance and team work. The walkers come from a wide variety of organisations with boys aged 15 walking a 35-mile route and youths of 16 and 17 covering 45 miles. Young men aged 18 and 19 hike 55 miles and girls walk 35 miles, although some can take longer routes.

Each team has 24-routes to choose from, but they must visit 10 tors in a certain order and they have to carry enough food to last for the two days as well as their tents and bedding. Times for completing the course can vary widely, but it is expected that the main group will return to the camp by 5 p.m. on Sunday.

Hundreds of Service men and women have given up their weekend to help to run the event. There will also be support from the Dartmoor Rescue Group, the police, the St. John Ambulance Brigade, volunteer doctors, nurses and others.

The expedition is organised by the Army's South West District Headquarters at Bulford Camp. There will also be support from the Royal Navy, the Royal Marines, and the Royal Air Force. A special one-day event is also being run for handicapped people. These will be tackling routes cross country or on army roads with support from volunteer helpers.

E2 Work together to complete this summary.

The Ten Tors Expedition takes place on .... every .... The competitors walk in teams of .... people. They wear .... and they must carry .... , ... and .... with them. They walk .... , ... or 55 .... , according to their age.

In 1983 .... started the course but more than .... couldn't finish because the .... was very bad. One boy had to go to hospital by .... when a gas cylinder .... in his tent. There were a lot of .... with .... on their feet and .... ankles. The 'winners' were the .... combined cadet force, the group called .... from Exeter, and RAF ....

Beaten by Dartmoor

One boy was burned and harsh weather forced more than 450 other youngsters to drop out of the 24th annual Ten Tors expedition on Dartmoor at the weekend.

Ronald Wheeler, aged 15, a member of the Eastbourne Sea Cadets team was burned when a gas cylinder he was using in a tent exploded after his team had set up camp at Rough Tor, near Postbridge.

He was taken by a Wessex helicopter to the Royal Naval Hospital, Plymouth, where he is expected to stay for two days.

A young man, who had been flown on Saturday back to the medical centre at Okehampton Camp, suffering from hypothermia, left the centre yesterday after treatment.

The other casualties were mainly youngsters with blisters and twisted ankles.

The army, which organises the expedition, says the Ten Tors is a test of endurance. Exeter Schools' combined cadet force was first home in the 35-mile section, a group from Exeter called Operation Dartmoor was first home in the 45-mile section, and RAF Halton was first home on the 55-mile route.

20 MEMORY SEARCH 20

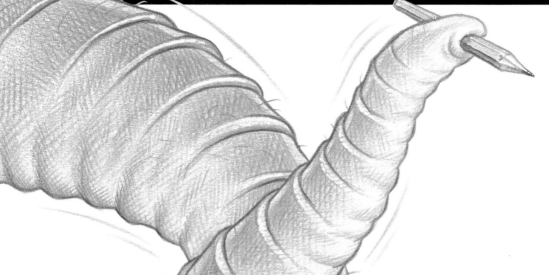

A Quiz

How much do you remember? The answers are all in this book.

1 Which group of people sailed from Plymouth in 1620?

2 When is Bonfire Night?

3 What are the 'five aches'?

4 Who wrote *The Road to Wigan Pier*?

5 Name three national newspapers on sale in Britain.

6 How old must you be before you can buy beer in a pub?

7 What is a 'licensed' hotel?

8 What happened on June 2, 1953?

9 What do English people often eat at Christmas?

10 What is January 1st called?

11 Name five items of unisex clothing.

12 Where do you go if you lose a scarf on the train?

13 What number do you dial if you see a bank robbery?

14 What do English people sometimes eat with roast beef?

15 Which book tells you about motoring laws in Britain?

B Talking about your English course

Work in small groups. Discuss these questions.

1 What have you enjoyed most about your course?

2 What will you miss when you go home?

3 What are you looking forward to doing when you get home?

4 What will you remember when you get home?

Here are some ideas to help you:

C Buying presents

C1 Work in small groups. Discuss these questions.

1 Have you bought any presents?
2 What have you bought? Who are the presents for?
3 Do you think it is easy or difficult to choose presents for people?
4 Do you like receiving presents?
5 What presents would you like for your birthday?

C2 Mr Smythe has been round the world. He has bought some presents for his family.

Work in small groups. Decide who the members of the family are. Describe the presents, and find out their names. Then decide which country each present is from, and who Mr Smythe should give it to.

Discuss your decisions with the rest of the class.

94

D Goodbyes

D1 🔲 Pierre has been staying with his friends Alan and Carol.

Listen to the conversation and find the answers to these questions:

1 Where do you think Pierre is going?
2 What does he think of Carol's cooking?
3 Who can't he say goodbye to?

Pierre Well, it's time to go. The taxi's here.
Carol Yes, I hope you have a good journey. Don't forget to write, will you?
Pierre I'll write as soon as I get home. Thanks for everything.
Alan Not at all. We've enjoyed having you here.
Pierre I've had a fantastic time and you must come and stay with me some time.
Alan Yes, we'd love to.
Pierre I'll miss your excellent cooking!
Carol Thank you. I'm glad you liked it.
Alan Mm . . . but I'm sure you're looking forward to seeing your family again and eating French food!
Pierre Yes, I am. Well, goodbye then. Say goodbye to the children for me.
Carol We will. Bye, look after yourself!
Alan Give our best wishes to everyone!

D2 Read the conversation again and complete these sentences.

1 Pierre promises to . . .
2 He invites Alan and Carol to . . .
3 He says he'll miss . . .
4 He's looking forward to . . .
5 He wants Alan and Carol to . . .
6 Alan tells him to . . .

D3 Now *you* are leaving. What are you going to say? Fill the blanks.

It's time to . . .
Thanks for . . .
I'll . . .
I'll miss . . .
Say goodbye to . . . for me.
Give my best wishes to . . .
Don't forget to . . .
Well, goodbye . . .

E What would you say?

1 You are introduced to an old lady you do not know. What do you say?

2 You are in a strange town. You want to find the railway station. What do you ask the policeman?

3 You are in a restaurant. You'd like steak and chips. What do you say to the waiter?

4 You are leaving a party. The hostess says 'Goodbye'. What do you say?

5 You are in the cinema. You can't see the film because the lady in front of you is wearing an enormous hat. What do you say to her?

6 You are staying with a friend. You want to make a phone call. What do you say?

7 Your friend has a stomach upset. She doesn't know what to do. Give her some advice.

8 You are discussing sport with a friend. He says, 'I think everyone should play cricket.' What is your reply?

9 You want to invite a friend to a party. What do you say?

10 You are going out with a friend. She wants to go to the cinema but you don't want to see the film. You want to go to the theatre. What do you say?

11 Your friend says, 'You must come and stay with us this summer.' How do you reply?

12 You always enjoy staying with your aunt because she makes delicious cakes. Now you are leaving after a week's stay. What do you say?

13 Your aunt says, 'Don't forget to phone me.' How do you reply?

14 You want to buy a corkscrew but you've forgotten what it is called in English. What do you say to the shop assistant?

15 You've just spilt coffee on your landlady's carpet. What do you say?

16 The radio you bought yesterday doesn't work properly. You take it back to the shop. What do you say to the shop assistant?

17 Your friend has bought a car with no MoT. What do you say?

18 Your neighbour looks very happy. He says, 'We've just had twins!' What do you say?

19 Your friend is planning to go to Scotland by train. You think there may be a train strike. What do you say?

20 You're leaving from the airport. Your uncle is there but you didn't say goodbye to your cousins. What do you say to your uncle?

F Leaving

F1 In your groups, decide how to complete the song using the words given in the list.

Leaving on a Jet Plane (John Denver)

All my bags are ......, I'm ready to ......

I'm standing here ...... your door.

I ...... to wake you up to say ......

But the ...... is breaking, it's ...... morn'.

......'s waiting, he's ...... his horn

Already I'm so lonesome I could ......

goodbye
blowing
dawn
taxi
outside
packed
cry
early
go
hate

So ...... me and smile for me.

Tell me that you'll ...... for me.

Hold me like you'll never ...... me ......

'Cause I'm leaving on a jet plane,

Don't know when I'll be back ......

Oh babe, I hate to go.

again
go
kiss
let
wait

There's so many ...... I've let you ......

So many ...... I've played around.

I tell you now, they don't ...... a thing.

Every ...... I go, I'll ...... of you.

Every ...... I sing, I'll ...... for you.

When I ...., I'll ...... your wedding ......

ring
times
sing
mean
come
down
back
times
think
song
wear
place

Well now, the time ...... to leave you.

One more time, please let me ...... you.

Then close your eyes and I'll be ....

Dream about the days to come

When I won't .... you alone.

About the times, I won't ....

way
have to
leave
has come
on
have to
kiss
say
my

F2 🔲 Listen to the whole song. Discuss these questions:

1 What is the relationship between the two people in the song?
2 What does the singer promise?
3 How is she travelling?
4 How long will she be away?
5 What does she tell him to look forward to?
6 Why do you think she's leaving?